Another View of the City

Books by Russell Peterson

SILENTLY, BY NIGHT

ANOTHER VIEW OF THE CITY

Russell Peterson

Another View of the City

McGraw-Hill Book Company
New York · Toronto · London · Sydney

To my father, and to his old West Brook

Contents

Introduction

In between the umbilical networks of highway that link one metropolis with others of its kind are some quiet places virtually untouched by the frenetic contortions of progress. The traveller who streaks by in an airborne tube or uses the great turnpikes as a greased chute misses not a little in his headlong plunge.

The nearest sizable group of houses from where I am sitting, cross-legged in the aromatic leaves and warmed by a late October sun, is a small village. It has always been here, just down the road. Ancient Indian tribes used the spot for centuries before the Delaware Indians, from a height which begins where now the village boundary touches the woods, saw Henry Hudson drop anchor behind Sandy Hook. The British, retreating from the Battle of Monmouth, crossed through it in disarray as they sought rendezvous with their fleet. Its native sons have gone off to every war since American wars began. There is an old white house on a corner where used to stand a colonial tavern; there is a church—two churches; there is a school; a volunteer fire house; Albert Bullwinkel's house, and some others; and a general store in the corner of which is a small post office, complete with American flag and stamps, not only the hideous commemorative kind, but also those showing the strong, aquiline likeness of George Washington—who himself passed this way. A recent book describes this little hamlet as being "one of the lost towns of America." Someone is lost, well enough, but it is not this town. It is here, as I say, and blows its fire siren daily—a long, dreadful groan at noon.

We are close by the sea. The tide here has no great Fundy bore nor any perilous rips or races, nor any depth; it simply comes to us quietly, twice each day, as comfortably regular as the fire siren. Sneaking up the estuary into the creeks and purging the fresh-water streams with a salt gargle, the time comes, pauses, and slides back out again, swinging the red nun buoys round the other way as it goes. There are fingers of salt water, and coves, and a hundred shallows and pools in which tidal life abounds and is ceaselessly hunted out by the ever-watchful gulls and shore birds. Fishing is good, crabs are fat, and clams are in teeming abundance. There are salt marshes, narrow beaches of mud and shell and sand, water plants, and curious flotsam borne landward from the sea. It is a kindly shore, and safe.

Back beyond the tidemarks there are fresh streams and ponds, there are small meadows and capsule bogs, verdant gullies and cool, sweet springs. There are woods ("forests" has a more Northern ring) of tall oaks, tulip poplars, and maple. From the fragrant bay bushes on the tidal rim you can see billowing mounds of laurel, upland ferns, and hill-stones and wild azalea. Slipper orchids are common among the laurel burns; Lady's-tresses adorn the bank, not 30 feet from the salt water; and St.-John's-wort, trilliums, Bloodroot, and anemones are a thrown stick's distance from the edge of the salt marsh. Our hills above our sea are high. The highest is 400 feet. Someone will suggest that hills grow higher—and I will agree—but not, on this coast, between Maine and Mexico.

There are foxes in these woods, both Red and Gray—rather too many, in fact, for each spring they manage to make off with some of our best hens. There are skunks in considerable numbers and fat, waddling, impertinent raccoons. There are Gray squirrels, of course, and legions of busy mice, shrews, and moles. There are weasels and, yes, even mink. Bats, too, are here, cartwheeling through the twilight like silent toys. And although it sounds ridiculous, we can very nearly say—since our woods go down in places literally to arm's length from sea water—that there are even dolphins "in our woods." There are, however, no deer. The deer are gone, along with many another former inhabitant. There are other things, of course: chipmunks, possums, centipedes, salamanders, muskrats; legions of weevils, phalanxes of beetles, and cohorts of borers, ants, and spiders; there are wasps, bees, snakes, crayfish, turtles, periwinkles, horseshoe crabs, mushrooms, nuts, birds, frogs, and fishes. Though the last may sound like an overflowing from Aristophanes, these things are all very much alive, now, as I write; here, as I write. They are an inheritance, and some of this inheritance is here with us today, but many, one by one, are fading away and can never return.

The wild things about us are indeed leaving. Why? Because there is no place for them here except in pocket-sized islands of wilderness such as this, and even here they are being relentlessly pressed. If you should walk from the borders of the little village about which I spoke, and climb through the woods to the highest point, looking out over a great bay you would see the towers of New York not many miles distant. You would see, going out from that jagged granite pile rising above its oily tide, satellite piles reaching out as far as one can see. Only the blessed, growling ocean stops the relentless advance. I must firmly state that I am not against progress. I watched with quickened pulse the rising great pillars of steel of the Verrazano bridge as it emerged from its chrysalis, and view its finished span with awe and pride. I marvel at the sight of spear-points of jet aircraft across our home skies—and, oddly enough, they seem not out of place, so complete are they in beauty of form and movement. But in everyday life must all of our inheritance be obliterated?

The reason for this book is not to crusade but to relate quietly a chronicle of a country year—a country year within sight of New York City. Though a requiem is sounded, it is only for the past. The future holds what we will make of it.

Another View of the City

October

Vintage

A leaf beetle is hurrying somewhere, one wing askew; he looks ill-kept, as though summer was a toil and he yearns for the comfort of his winter retreat. There is an explosion of leaves from which I know will emerge a Towhee, for only he and the Fox sparrow, who has not yet come, can be so violent. Titmice are swarming over the old feeding tray, taking a sunflower seed and flying to a near branch to hammer it as lustily as a black-smith—then back to get another. There is a battered Mourning Cloak butterfly on a warm stone. There are no geese just now —although I heard them early this morning at dawn. But there are crows idly cawing—fish crows, for they have a strangled, adenoidal bleat, not a proper caw. There are hundreds of grackles reaping the harvest of dogwood berries, both berries and birds littering the road to make pleasing splashes of black and red on the yellow gravel. And there are Ring-billed gulls circling very high overhead, just idling on the hill thermals, I suppose, for certainly there is nothing for gulls in these oak woods.

It is October. And it is quiet now in the woods. But not many moments ago there was such a ringing of voices and stampeding of feet that even now you can almost hear the echoes still tumbling off the back porch and into the yard. There is a small-sized sneaker upside down among the leaves freshly fallen on the new rye grass. And although they are all well out of hearing, I can imagine I hear knife clicks and smell peanut butter and jam.

I have remained out here to rest. We spent the morning harvesting the last grapes and late apples. The children made a sport of batting the deadfalls, and we were all so covered with pulp and apple juice that the bees left the fallen apples to follow us. In such an overflow of high spirits someone managed to get stung, and while he howled another put his elbow through a kitchen windowpane, and I had to clamp down. Now, in the lull, I have time to notice the day itself. It is neither foul nor fair. There is a bluish haze and only a lukewarm sun, but there is that soft quality, in this most gossamer of light airs, which seems to wrap you in sensuous folds and accentuates the heady fragrance of leaf-reek and the peaty scents of autumn. We did not choose this day to do any special thing; you don't in the country. Here the days run so into each other that whole series of them are somehow lost.

October. It is a time-of-the-year, as there are stages to life. But, unlike life, times-of-the-year offer one another chance, a sort of annual reincarnation, a repeating of Time. If it rains at this year's Race Meet, there will be other years. There are a thousand ways to measure Time. Paleo-historians speak in eras and in multiples of millions of years. Electrophysicists sort and divide microseconds. But however it may be counted, Time is important to us. Days are too short, and are seemingly gone before they begin. And weeks are just omelets of days. A month is a measure more suited to man than any other. Only a month gives a man time to stretch, to kick stones with the toe of his boot, to wait out wet days, and to lie in the sun at full length and watch clouds go by. And October is as good a month as any if beginnings are to be made.

Why anyone chose to "begin" the year with January is difficult to see. Climate and locale and, particularly, the idiosyncrasies of calendar-makers are all factors to be considered. But January, even in Italy, is low, mean, and brooding, not to mention being two-faced into the bargain. April would be more proper, surely, or at least some part of spring, in which rebirth and awakening is a promise if not actually in evidence. Or why not November for this beginning one must have? November is certainly a time for holing up, battening down, or fleeing from a wrathful season that is nearly upon us. But I choose October as a time for beginning: first, because it happens, as I say, to *be* October (and is thus simply well-washed and cleanly logical); and last, because here—a specific place at a specific point in Time—October is the vintage of the year. Our year—our own year here at home, I mean—in its slow-flowering way to maturity under a hot summer sun, seems to advance to such a bursting fullness of harvest bounty that one is left in a state of exhaustion, replete and stupefied. For the year's end— October—is a time when not only harvest spills, as do apples in thunderous cadence from a hogshead barrel, down upon us, but in all things this peak of vintage prevails. Scents are more deeply aromatic, and even the breeze is softer, more caressing. Sounds carry further, and are muted in the smoky haze. And the sight —as of a paint shop gone suddenly mad—of leaves rioting in glorious excess of color and form is an elixir nearly too strong for orderly absorption by one's mind. The burgeoning cornu- copia of fruit, of scent, of sound, and of color, and magnitudi- nous beneficence in weather and well-being, is all upon us in a deluge.

Then, of a sudden, as though a gong were sounded, it is all over. To the physical senses there appears no change. But within our inner being it is as though a chill wind had softly, just once, blown through summer's curtain. One shudder from within and the play is ended. The last act is played out in panoply and grandeur, but our hero is dead of a cold blade through the heart.

But before "exit October" is borne to us by that fatal wind there is a thunderous roar from the upper tiers: the grackle in- vasion is upon us with a thrust and force that is deafening.

Grackles are large blackbirds, long of tail, bright of eye, radiantly iridescent in sheen, static in movement, and impressively noisy of mouth. At their first arrival, in conservative foraging parties, their presence, as I have mentioned, is not only tolerable but welcomed, as an animate and colorful addition to the backdrop of autumn's plenty. There seems room for all. And in great good humor we, as it were, fall-to waving in everyone and everything with welcoming gestures. But one day there seems to be a ruffling of discord. Then a swelling of discord. Finally we are jarred from our benignity by what seems a whirlwind of cacophony. Grackles are everywhere in screaming legions. They darken the sky in uncounted thousands, descending as shimmering blankets upon the fruit-laden dogwoods and other berry-bearing trees. Within minutes the trees are perilously distorted under the weight of noisy, quarrelsome bodies and are quickly denuded and left barren of their beauty. Contagious panic, whim, or perhaps some innate urge suddenly uncoiled brings an abrupt end to both plunder and vocal harassment, and, as a body, the thousands ascend in a roar and tumult that pelts the air as might a scattering of explosive debris. Then they are but a vague hum on the horizon, a waxing and waning murmur, soon to fade into silence . . . until, with another great rush of violence and wild disorder, a fresh horde will descend like a mortar barrage upon whatever remains standing and gives evidence of being even vaguely edible.

While the days are filled with energy and brilliance, October nights are calm and liberally given to periods of near silence and reflective peace. Nights are often warm and wrapped in an aura of aromatic pungency; but as often they are cool, antiseptic, lacking sensory attributes, suggestive of the sterile void that is to come. On such nights, coming clearly and starkly through the metallic crispness, the whip-clear call of the Whippoorwill will frequently be heard. The Whippoorwill is most drably dressed and, being nocturnal, is scarcely a common sight. But its voice, though loudly declarative and crisply punctuated, falls sweetly on the ear. The treble night cry of our "whip-poor-will" is sharply given, with emphasis on the "whip." Similar species in other climes have a much softer call. It would seem as though the ring of early ice were echoed in our bird. In the heavy, close heat of mid-August nights the Whippoorwill's cry seems to many to have a hint of melancholy and even a mournful quality. But to us in October it rings with the clarity of bell metal.

"Living in the country" is not quite the same as "country living." But in either case a definition of "country" is altogether necessary. "Country" is not a thing in itself, as is "wilderness." "Country" implies—and indeed must have—an apposite. That apposite is, of course, the city. The two must always not only be comparable, but adjacent, for one is in direct relation to the other. The perpetual shuffling of values and concepts among those who, generation leading to generation, are in positions of planning and building continually denies open expanse and natural beauty to the urban dwellers, and facilities and adequacy of means to those living in more open adjacent areas. Soon an enforced compromise must be brought about or one will surely destroy the other. In either case (that of wilderness devastated or cities in ruins), both will lose.

I have tried, by way of introductory notes, to describe this particular corner of the world in which the pageantry of country life revolves. But being introductory, my descriptive range was necessarily restricted and, certainly, beyond a doubt, not a little poetic in its approach. In fact, my phrases on the beauty, the settled composure of the scene, the generally quiet harmony of its inhabitants—in a word, the classically idyllic landscape— would, if continued in such a vein, be quite enough to assault one's sensitivities. But such a paean, at the same time, is altogether an accurate description: it *is* that way. The joy of life and the beauty of life are very real, a very great part of living here. But this is not Walden Pond. At one time it might well have been, but not now. The escalatory pace of our modern world has quickened to the tempo of a machine gone mad. This quiet corner is a backwater—actually a freak, an eddy temporarily isolated from the lunging river of Progress. Although we call it country living, it is truly only another view of the city. The "country" is near, now, just further beyond, still adjacent—but we, here, are already encompassed. It is in this realization that some small hope for survival is to be seen. It is still just possible that instead of being seen as a part of the city too fragile to survive, it could happen—as the eleventh hour fast approaches —that the existence of such backwaters as ours be recognized as the spawning ground of true fulfillment in urban existence.

To be geographically specific, this vest-pocket Eden lies behind Sandy Hook on the northeastern, coastal edge of the state of New Jersey. It is remarkable in the fact that, since the eastern coast of the United States is well known to be monotonously flat from New England to Florida, the hills which lie behind Sandy Hook are, first of all, the only hills of any kind intruding upon this great, flattened expanse of coast; and secondly, they actually abut the sea, coming nearly straight down in steep, wooded cliffs. How Englishmen, with their great southern cliffs of massive chalk and their wave-smashed northern coast, would hoot at our pipsqueak "hills going down to the sea." One can hear the loud and derisive laughter of Oregonians! It is true that the "immense" height of our hills is scarcely 400 feet—little higher than can be reached by a batted ball—but to us they are of value, they have stature, and they are, in a word, eminently satisfactory.

Sandy Hook in itself is no mere sand strip. It is not just that its crooked finger juts out and makes a boundary for one of the greatest harbors in the world, and it is not only that, historically speaking, it has had role after dramatic role in the formation and defense of this country. It is, or it seems, far superior to the mundanely anchored and stone-dead qualities of other landscapes, for ours has a virtual animation. It actually does "move." A recently published series of maps, covering nearly two centuries, shows how Sandy Hook opens, closes, bends, and contorts; becoming a peninsula, then an island, then again a peninsula. At the moment it is a barrier peninsula—but quite another kind of peninsula than it was a reasonably short number of years ago. But with all its flighty tendencies to wander about, Sandy Hook faithfully remains with us. And even beyond that, it holds great interest in the variety and scope of both its flora and fauna, many being things apart from varieties found on the mainland.

Our principal body of water is the gray and restless Atlantic, which is held—or more-or-less held—from us by the Sandy Hook barrier beach. She is always with us, in both sight and sound. We feel her clean, cold breath at all hours and, depending on the direction of the wind, we hear her constant voice either grumbling or snarling in staccato rage. She is seldom silent.

On the northerly side of the Highlands massif, in generally quiescent mood (since it too is west of Sandy Hook), lies Sandy Hook Bay. And on the south—our side—spreads the Shrewsbury River—also called the Navesink. It is not really a "river" at all, although a few tributorial rivulets do timidly enter into its great expanse; and, perhaps, under the middle-grade standards of "official" nomenclature, it does pass as a river. What it *is*, however, is a tidal estuary of singular beauty and no mean strength to its pull. It is lined with pebbles and sand over most of its reaches, but there are some areas also of appallingly viscous, leaden-black mud.

The land masses here, with the exception of the striking Highlands, are relatively unremarkable. The inconsequential heights of land eastward of the Raritan basin slope off toward the sea in a dreary series of minor hill formations, wooded gullies, and rolling fields. It is difficult to envision the primordial abundance of forest trees, because this great alluvial plain has been under constant cultivation for nearly as long as any other single spot in this hemisphere. Only on some of the oldest of pre-colonial Dutch farmsteads does one find, upon rare occasions, some of the great, gnarled White pines, last remnants of the original forest cover. To the southward, not far beyond a final, contorted ripple of small hills, there opens out as in a gesture of splendor the seemingly limitless expanse of the Pine Barrens.

It is here, then, in the midst of such surroundings, that we live, clutched round by the Highlands like a small sparrow cupped in protective hands. Our lovely road—really little more than a lane—reaches down to within a yard or two of the salt water. There is an oak woods on one side and a tulip poplar *cum* holly woods on the other. There is a fresh-water stream—two—one of which empties into a small marsh that is distinctive in being fresh marsh on the higher end and salt marsh on the lower. The other stream flows into a fresh-water pond, which, in turn, flows over a small weir into the tidal salt. It is a strange and wonderful feeling of contrasts to see that while, say, fishing for Small-mouthed bass from the road, one's lure, if dropped down behind, would frighten shrimp and very possibly disturb a Bluefish.

Columbus Day has recently been on the rack. It seems that Leif Ericson got here first. Good enough, if you will have it that way—it's probably quite true. But personally, I am most vehemently pro-Italian and in every way Italo-oriented. Columbus Day may not mean much in Pueblo, Colorado, but in New Jersey there are many Italians, and Italians insist that one have Columbus Day off—"off" (in local parlance) meaning "no work." Thus, all during my boyhood this day has been a holiday, and a holiday falling (unlike freezing Christmas or the baking Fourth of July) at exactly the crown of the year: soft and generous October. So hurrah for *Cacciucco alla Livornese*, hurrah for Carlo Giuseppe Vacca (who is a friend of mine), and hurrah for Christopher Columbus. *È buono.*

It was on Columbus Day, recently, when my notebook recorded the following data: "It is exactly one o'clock P.M.; the wind is slight, SSW; temperature 78°; humidity 48 per cent; barometer 29.85, falling." Now this sounds like so much trivia, and it is. But my reason for writing it down was that the day was, to me, so completely perfect I felt something must be done to record it. It was a day not all that "clear"; it was, in fact, rather in between. Days of definite and irradicable foulness or

fairness seems always, somehow, to stir the blood and be con-
ducive to action. But days like this one are lulling to a degree
of being almost bewitched, having a quality incomprehensible,
yet so tangible it seems to be sensed and felt—as if one might roll
it between one's fingers, or stroke it, like a cat. Such days are
the same in this quality regardless of season.

On this particular Columbus Day the air was of a delicate
softness and the breeze was a median of all breezes: a breeze
neither to push, buffet, nor chill; neither warm nor cooling.
Rather than blowing at or round you, it wrapped you in a
caress. There was a haze, and, at best, a lukewarm sun.

On this day I went for a sail. My boat was a New Jersey boat.
She was cat-rigged with a gaff, of extremely shallow draft,
exactly 15 feet in length and 5½ in beam, and very, very old.
Her class bore the odd name of "Barnegat Bay Sneak Box"—
thus called since she was sailed in summer for pleasure, then
dismasted and used, because of her low silhouette, as a floating
platform from which to shoot waterfowl in winter. She was
aptly named after a local goose: her name was *Brant*.

As I sailed past Fair Haven and on to Red Bank, my little boat
behaved with her usual stability and trustworthiness. I passed
other sailboats, all more grand than we, and motor launches and
fishing boats. I passed by people crabbing in rowboats, although
crabs are scarce this late in the year. The remains of someone's
lunch floated by, and I scowled. And in the secluded backwater
of McClee's Creek, I saw a wild goose.

At Red Bank there was a sudden, brief surge of wind and
my starboard stay snapped. I was hard put to save the mast.
But I turned into the wind and doctored the turnbuckle with
some marlin, which held, downwind, on the way home. I dined
rather ingloriously on a jelly sandwich and a pear. There may
be a question of the relevancy of that—and, for that matter, of
the entire day's summation; for nothing happened, nothing at
all. It was simply that I felt keenly that I was very much alive.
And I gave a prayer for that day, Columbus being thrown in
for good measure.

Having seen a goose brings us to geese. Here on a coastal waterway close by the sea, geese are to be reckoned with. I do not mean they become a problem in themselves; but their presence does face us with and waken in us that certain feral quality hidden within most, if not all, of us. There is my point. There are many things wild and untamed, but a wild goose somehow *seems* wild. Surely it is connected, somehow, with a "majestic" quality of freedom in flight. One need have no underlying psychological aberration to deeply comprehend, not without envy, the grandeur and ecstasy of free flight. It is most natural for our minds to fly "as the wild goose flies." It is upward and away; a quick, clean escape from the mundane. The great ordered wedges of geese in flight are a common sight on the New Jersey coast. They are more readily to be seen in secluded backwaters of littoral water, in estuaries and inlets and in salt-water ponds. But they are often seen as well, singly or in small groups, even in the most uninviting of back country sinkholes or bog water. But it is to the salt estuaries, fresh with the tang of the sea, that they are drawn in any numbers.

"Wild goose," in eastern North America, commonly refers to the Canada goose, certainly a magnificent bird. And in New Jersey we have numbers of these wildfowl: it is they who fly high and pound down the flyways; it is they who are the most noble and best of all American wildfowl. But even more intimately associated with coastal New Jersey is the considerably less spectacular Brant. The American Brant is a cousin of the European "Brent goose," as its seemingly plagiarized name would suggest. It is a true maritime goose, being most infrequently seen far from the reaches of salt water. The Brant seems niggardly and skulking by comparison with the vibrant Canadian. He seems stupid, dwarfed, and dull—again, by comparison. But it is not by comparison that he is known along the Jersey coastal marshes. In a purely local way he is "one of us," and is loved for himself.

Certainly not spectacular, the Brant has yet a certain beauty of his own. He is quite exceptionally dark and is small, goosewise (being more nearly the size of a Mallard). The head and neck are of a leaden, lackluster black, without the proud white blaze of the Canadian honker and having in its place but a mere afterthought of four small white lines which form an inadequate and broken crescent. The tail is not excessively short but the rather long "tail coverts" (those armor-like fans of short feathers above and beneath the tail itself) make it seem so; the resulting appearance being a rump rather high out of the water, with just a line of black for a tail.

In our local scene the Brant fits most comfortably into a season which finds our estuary cold, silent, and little filled with any real activity outside the ubiquitous gulls. But the Brant is not entirely, as we prefer to think, "our own." It is easy enough to say "our own" or "one of us," but such usage is often very deceptive. The Brant first sees daylight on the still-frozen tundra of Baffin Island. It is by birth a bird of the steel-blue Arctic waters and knows in its youth only barren rocks, lichens, and the company of Eider ducks. But growing maturity and the autumnal advent of bitter cold and perpetual darkness sets him on a southward exodus. New Jersey is not his only wintering ground—he goes well into North Carolina—but it is among his principal ones. He remains a "northern" bird; seldom, except through extreme happenstance, does he penetrate to Florida. Thus, although he is not entirely our own, to say he is "ours" is not wholly inaccurate, for during a considerable portion of the year he not only remains with us but becomes a part of our seascape.

Our own cove, our own estuary—although seldom without Brant in some part of their wide expanses—are not the principal wintering quarters for these birds. One must go southward, but only about thirty miles. It is in Barnegat Bay that the Brant yields to none, both in numbers and in exquisite beauty of form and flight. Although he is small and short-necked, the Brant is a particularly long-winged and agile goose. It has been said that no ducks or geese can compare with them for sheer beauty of movement. On the water they are poised as daintily and as buoyantly as are gulls. They feed most gracefully, pivoting and whirling with something akin to the phalarope's zest. But it is in flight that they become a thing apart. Brant do not generally fly in V-shaped flocks, as do Canada geese, but in irregular groups or in long lines. They fly low in undulating procession, much more swiftly than they appear to do. They often wheel in unison, changing from a dull black line into a flashing burst of white as their flanks are caught by the sunlight; another turn, and they are dark again. Vacillating, dark to light and light to dark, they may suddenly turn, as a necklace flung skyward, and fly at a great height; then back they will fall to within inches of the choppy waves, all still in a line but waving like a reed before the wind.

The principal food of the American Brant is Eelgrass (*Zostera marina*). But they do not graze on dry land, as other geese, nor do they dive, but wait for the tide to uncover the waving beds of their favorite marine plant. They would seem to pull up more of the plants than they could possibly eat, preferring the white roots and stalk, but eating the green parts as well. They feed as long as the tide permits them to reach down by "tipping" (as do the surface-feeders among ducks), then they consume the floating grasses previously uncovered and uprooted. They seldom ignore mollusks and other tidal delicacies, but their preference is for Eelgrass. When, in 1931, Eelgrass suffered a blight and was nearly obliterated on much of the Brant's feeding grounds, this goose decreased to only a fifth of its usual numbers. Now the Eelgrass is returning, and the Brant is growing in numbers with it.

Shooting Brant on Barnegat Bay has been a favored sport for nearly as long as the area has been known. Their flesh is exceptionally well-flavored and firm, and they remain a perennial favorite of the native hunters along the Jersey shore.

But geese other than Brant come over our woods and splash into our protected cove. Last winter I walked from the barn to the water's edge to investigate a muskrat which was behaving queerly (it had, I found, only two and a half legs; the rest hav-

ing been lost in traps). I was able to reach within a few feet of the injured animal before it managed (quite adeptly, I thought) to slide across the mud and into the water, where its strong bladelike tail greatly helped its pitiful progress. But my stealth in muskrat-watching was well rewarded, for, as I slowly regained my feet, after having knelt in the protected lee of some reeds, I saw, not many yards away, a small flock of Greater Snow geese, bobbing and preening on the choppy blue water. They are wholly white but for their black primary feathers, and are always a stirring sight. Upon rare occasions a Blue goose is seen in these waters, but never in numbers. The Western White-fronted goose is noted with even less frequency. It seems strange that the Greater Snow goose should be so seldom seen here, for New Jersey is host to thousands of Snow geese with, even, an occasional intermixed Blue goose at Fortescue on Delaware Bay, little more than a hundred miles further south. And of course there comes, upon infrequent occasion, the true rarity, the storm-tossed or otherwise lost traveller from abroad: the errant Barnacle goose or Greylag from Europe. But however many we may see of our pampered Brant, or any other varieties, it is still the magnificent Canada goose which most stirs us. It is only he, who, full-throated, strong, and unwearying, carries away the mind. The great wedges of these geese, flying in tempo with the seasons, are ever a renewal of hope and a promise of continuity.

Have we not a surfeit of geese? I should think so. But I feel urged to mention yet one more. Coming home from hill or tidal shoreline, there is one goose more faithful and more enduring than any of the rest. She is so old her head is quite white. But she is not infirm. Nor is she—geese are prone to be—a goose of wrath, ill-judgment, and even more ill-considered aggression. She is a good goose, and kind. She is a Toulouse goose, the gray barnyard kind, and has no name but "goose"—except that the children often call her by the nursery rhyme name, "Waggle-tail-loose." She is staunch, steady, courageous to a fault. Her eye, cocked skyward, sees the hawk before it can be seen with binoculars. Her wings beating the air and her great trumpet of a cry are a warning to all fowls—to all men—that the barnyard is not aright. She gives no pusillanimous alarums; when she sounds out in earnest it is a peril very real indeed—at least as real and as true as good goosely judgment can ascertain it to be. She greets me in the early dawn with a torrent of welcome, and answers my replies with even greater volume and exclamatory expostulation. She will, it is true, untie one's shoelaces. But she never, never bites. She rubs her bill on one's leg, nibbles a bit caressingly, and bends her head to be scratched. She welcomed me this evening in the late afternoon; didn't have much to say, just followed me up the path. She is sitting now, on the front porch, silently contemplating me through the screen door. She is not allowed in the house—nor even, come to think of it, on the porch. We love her with an abiding affection. But her eliminatory processes are timed by intricacies of computation far beyond the reckoning of mere mortals. So she must ever remain an exile, outside.

Enough of geese.

I have mentioned migration. Somehow it always seems more immense and powerful a thing in the autumn. In spring the birds seem to wander back more casually, as though dragging their feet in getting down to the hard work of nesting and raising families. Fall migrations come at the signal of weather. A clear harvest moon and a wind from out of the north brings flight upon flight of birds winging their way southward along the coastal Atlantic flyway.

They are of all types and varieties, but generally they group together; even among the more solitary kinds, such as warblers and sparrows, there will be inroads of identical birds, such as, say, all Magnolia warblers or all Swamp sparrows. The "flocking varieties," such as swallows and blackbirds, one might well expect to find together. But these generally leave quite early— long before migration would seem to have begun. They are with us by thousands one day, and completely gone the next. But among the warblers, one might go all spring and summer without seeing a certain kind, then suddenly—and often in one tree —see a dozen or more. It is true that they are more drab in their autumnal plumage, but their presence is always welcome.

Along the narrow barrier beach which runs from Sandy Hook all the way to the mainland at Long Branch, there lies a road. Between the road and the crashing Atlantic there is only a sea wall, the beach having been nearly obliterated along much of that section. The wall has recently been shored up with concrete, but for many years the massive boulders were often shifted and thrown about during storms; some hurled, even, into the road beyond, while the sea swept in to flood and harass the residents so dependent on the wall's brute strength. Even now great waves smash upward and over this wall, drenching cars with salt spray. Parallel to the road and to the sea wall, and on the seaward side, there is a tall rank of utility poles, high, ugly, disappearing off into the south. It is these poles which constitute the villain in the story I have to relate.

Along the coastal flyway there are great gaps. One is Block Island Sound; another, New York Bay; yet another, the Chesapeake, and so on. In flying southward, birds generally have good, firm land beneath. Thus, in event of a storm or sudden reversal of winds, they can quickly spiral downward and seek the shelter of bush or tree until the trouble is past. Only where they must cross open water does stark danger threaten. If they should tire there is nothing to save them outside of the rigging of a passing ship. They can only drop into the cold sea and die. But most struggle on—often forced perilously close to the waves, but somehow beating ever southward until landfall appears. Under certain adverse conditions the low bushes of Sandy Hook are all they can hope for, and they fall into these in a dazed state, wings askew, and poor heads ruffled and drooping.

There is a particular section of the beach area, below Sandy Hook, known to be the lowest section of the strip—nearly at sea level. The sharp rise of the Highlands, with its twin-towered

lights, lies just behind the narrow, tide-swept belt of water between. For some reason, it is at this spot that thousands of small
birds seem to arrive straight (it seems) off the ocean. Actually,
they fly from, perhaps, the Long Island coastal strips above New
York Bay; but some very likely come to us even from maritime
Rhode Island or from Martha's Vineyard.

They are tired as they approach land. Very tired, and flying
now with far less strength and showing none of the vigor which
they must have shown as they launched themselves into their
ocean crossing. As they sweep in they must sense (if they cannot see it; for many, if not most, fly at night) the sea wall and
the proximity of land. What they cannot sense is the force of
updraft with which the wind strikes the wall and is thrown upward. Into this fierce funnel the birds are swept—up and over
the wall—but directly into the long row of lethal wires. They
are blown into the wires with such force that many are killed.
Night after night they are killed outright or fall dazed into the
paths of cars and are crushed beneath the wheels. Theories have

been stated which blame the blinding lights of the many cars for this slaughter, but they are wrong in this case; here the damage is done before the birds fall to the road.

I have come by of an early October morning to find upwards of three hundred warblers, sparrows, vireos, thrushes, catbirds —even a Wilson's snipe, a King rail, and a gallinule. There are robins, wrens, kinglets, and shrikes. All thrown together as though pitched from the Ark. On other mornings there have been all Savannah sparrows—and on another little else but Gray-cheeked thrushes. One morning, along but two measured miles of road there were over two hundred dead birds. I collected sixty-five which were virtually untouched. They were of all kinds. I took a picture of them and wrote of the exact nature of their end for an ornithological group. There were exclamations of horror, and later, when a newspaper registered a more widely read account, there were angry letters of complaint. Someone suggested that the poles be moved—but someone, I am certain, unaffected by the immense cost involved. The poles will remain. The birds will die. I can think of no answer.

Generally during the last week of each October there is that which, to me, is the high point of the year's activities. It is the annual Race Meet. The proceeds donated to local charities, it is a very much countrified affair of horses racing for prize cups and assorted silverware. The course is over brush and timber obstacles in what is called "steeplechasing." The days are not always fair—though at that season they usually are—but whatever the weather, the races go on anyway.

The day of the Race Meet brings as many as 2,000 people into the hills behind the Navesink. Entrance is cheap. There is a band playing stirring marches, bunting, a great striped tent with refreshments, people milling about industriously laying down tartan blankets and spreading baskets of lunch. Dogs bark, children run back and forth, horns blow, eggs are eaten, whisky is drunk, and there is not one unhappy face anywhere. Bets are made, the horn sounds, and "they are off." Five races, generally.

The pounding of hooves, the din—is immense. The band still plays. Hats are flung into the air. There are cheers and applause.

Then it is all over. Everyone files off the course and the day ends. Often there are parties and dinners, and the spirit of the day is carried on into the night. Altogether it is a delightful, breathless, superbly beautiful kind of day. And every year, never failing, it returns to us with no shade of vigor diminished.

November

Wood Fires and Northern Lights

It would seem only proper that the first of November should begin with a howling Nor'easter. Has it not seemed cloying to have talked so much during October of "idyllic" days? Certainly it has. You can be thankful, no doubt, that you were spared "halcyon" nights! Surely too much saccharine sticks in one's throat, as does a surfeit of anything. But I have just come in through the front door—"blown in" would be more accurate —and I, for one, already miss October's balm, sugar-dipped or not. For two days now there has been a near gale out of the northeast. We are as snugly protected from storm as one could imagine, even from the dreaded Nor'east; but this storm seems to come straight down, as a hammer striking an anvil. With its first blast two of our hens were literally blown into a dogwood and had to be plucked out and unceremoniously thrown into their house. They squawked all the way but even their protests were swept away by the wind. The rain is still fiercely raging and forces itself in sheets through the thick oaks. It hammered and shook the house at first, but now has settled into a steady roar. And the weather has become chill. Not cold: not yet. But this is as far from last week's golden October as one can imagine. It is like dropping out of the sunlight and into a pit.

Such storms as this each year bring our thoughts to erosion. Not that we are at all affected here, as I have said, nor even (except for tidal damage) in any part of our estuary. But our barrier beach is so very vulnerable that scarcely any storm passes without leaving some scar. Of course, the solstice hurricanes are the worst, but a good, virile Nor'easter is no small thing to be passed over. Were it not for the intensity of the wind and rain we would hear the surf. Tomorrow, perhaps, or whenever the storm abates, we shall hear it, like a continuous dull ache, never relenting until the storm is days past.

Whatever we shall do when this great storm does finally blow out, I do not know. But one thing is certain: we shall all do it together. For the one great boon to the children after this forced confinement is to "survey the damage," and the real delight is in beachcombing. All manner of things are to be found as we, in a straggling company, patrol the narrow beach strip and the rock jetties. The surf still booms and we become damp with spray and encrusted with salt. The diamond-clear, cold salt air reddens noses, moistens eyes, and puts the spring of youth into even the most unlikely candidate (myself). And the beach is strewn with fresh mollusks and crabs, bits of sand-worn colored glass, brass fittings from torn and battered sections of boats, unusual fishes swept up from the depths, dead sea birds, whitened bones and curiously hooked piscine teeth, and marine animals and plants in a jumbled profusion. Last year, I remember, there were dozens of a clam strange to us: a round, flattened white mollusk the children identified as *Dosinia discus*, but "the book" was insistent upon Virginia's being its northernmost penetration. What it really was we shall never know, for we gathered them all and ate them. Somehow, it seemed like swallowing evidence, for, although shells were kept, time went by and they were somehow lost. Whatever it was, they tasted good enough. In fact, so fresh and clean seemed everything that day that we went on a "tasting binge." Razor clams, mussels, periwinkles, as well as our favorite Littlenecks, *Venus mercenaria*, and the common softshell *Mya arenaria*—all were sampled, some with hesitation and trepidation, others (the familiar ones) with huge gusto. The children kept the shells of the various kinds we ate or at least tasted. Only a few weeks ago I came upon a half-dozen old shells in the recess of a drawer: "ATE THIS" was inscribed in bold capitals in blue crayon.

I have spoken of the annual Race Meet, and of this still being "horse country." Do you know much of horses? If you should answer "very little," we are *simpatico* in this vast field of interest. And I say "vast" for it is, you know: horses are popular in America, and increasingly more and more people are becoming able to afford their care and the handling which they demand.

What does one *do* with a horse? The animal is fed and watered and curried and brushed; it is vacuum-cleaned, given shoes, and has its nails cleaned. Further, it is led, driven, or sat upon. Occasionally it is given to biting. And one kicked me once—squarely in the rump—and sent me galley west. This is all that I previously knew about horses; now I still say I know "very little," but I know considerably more than I did.

There is, in the countryside round about, that which is called a "Hunt." I had known of its presence, for upon occasion of a Saturday there would be a great hullabaloo of dog voices waxing and waning on the still air; and it had happened that profusely sweating, scarlet-faced men, mounted on equally lathered and highly odoriferous horses, came crashing through our woods in a riot of disorder. In one instance one of the leaders (I had taken him for such, for he carried a great whip and cursed most splendidly) came squarely up before our door and dismounted with a bound. He was beautifully attired in a hard, black velvet cap, white breeches, and a long woolen coat of dark green with, upon its collar, yellow and red tabs—seemingly an insigne of some sort. How the dark green shone against the white of his breeches! How his black and tan boots glistened! But how he stank! He smelled of sweating horse from yards away. And, I noticed, his lovely clothing was dripping wet, stained, and obviously badly rent by twig and brier.

Nearly before he struck the ground I enquired (somewhat icily between my teeth—for his horse's rear was planted firmly in among one of my japonicas, and its hind feet kept beating a tattoo among the bruised branches), "Can you be wanting something?" (I was not being at all nice.)

Before he said a word he noticed his horse in the bush and straightaway pulled it out, not without difficulty, for the animal seemed most fond of my bush and loathe to leave. All the while the rider voiced apologies in every direction, and in a manner laden with such charm and genuine embarrassment over his horse's lack of consideration, that I was quite prone to listen— although the animal had, by then, come perilously close to treading on my foot. The man was, he said, looking for a fool dog— lost, he indicated, as fool dogs are inclined to get. Had I seen him? No. Then off he would be; he mounted in a graceful arc and was in a moment clattering down the road in a swirl of dust, loose stones, and considerable glory. I waved and watched in no little awe and amusement as he waved back; but in his turning to wave, his mount gave an off-balance jog, and the seat of the gentleman's pants rose to a point of obvious danger above the saddle. But down he came safely; then, off he went at right angles to the road, crashing through the laurel tangles with the fury of a summer storm. A catbird came out to sit on the broken japonica.

Since that time I had heard various discussions concerning hunting, for a number of our friends were avid in their pursuit of this sport. I generally did not join in with the little knots of enthusiasts and was not pressed to, for they knew, or had the wisdom to surmise, that my sympathies would lie far more heavily with the fox. For in hunting (and "hunting," in our community, is far different from "shooting") there must be a fox. It was borne upon me that the distinction in phraseology was one of social segregation, but as I neither "hunted" nor did I "shoot" at anything anyway, by way of "sport," I was content to remain oblivious. With neither warring faction of fox-killers did I have much sympathy (my friends were quite right). I had

my arguments in plenty with foxes, but I preferred to settle them in my own way. I did notice, however, as I could hardly avoid, being so often in the thick of hunting conversations, that, although the avowed purpose of the sport was bloody enough, it was an infrequent fox whose brush and ears dangled from the stirrup thong of the sanguine victors. To me, there seemed to be far more chasing than catching, and it turned out that I was right.

You will notice that I perhaps seem casual and just a little callous and, even, superior, in my detachment from these hearty devotees of blood sport. It was just so, in the beginning. And I tell it to you from the beginning that you may not, later, mistake my position in all this. My ethereal detachment ended in this way.

On one day of completely idyllic dimension, warm, with a sky of pale, powder blue swept with only a wisp of cloud, I received a telephone call from a good friend. This friend was —and remains—one of our best commercial illustrators, whose work is sought after by every manner of editor and publisher. His problem, he said, was that he must have good photographs of horses charging about in every direction, as in battle, and did I know anything of the local hunting people. I explained the nature of my own ignorance, but said I might be able to come up with something. Another telephone call gave us the information that a hunt was being held that very afternoon, that at the moment dogs and horses were being set ready at the stables of a well-known estate, and that we were most welcome to go by. Within minutes we were there and in the center of goings-on which, to us, were as colorful as the panoply and dash of regimental review. Riders in green coats were wheeling and dashing up to a dust-scattering stop; then, turning, they would be off again and going. The women were dressed in coats of deep black and were as comely and attractive as I could ever have imagined; and their chestnut, bay, or black horses glistened and rippled under trappings of richly polished leather. The ladies' white gloves and breeches caught the light and lent sparkle and dash to their somber dress—as a diamond shines on the jeweller's velvet. There were some forty dogs—harriers—all rather splendid-looking, long-legged, and strong, as they milled, mingled, and scrambled for canine positions of prominence. Altogether it was a scene of glorious vigor, and both Stanley and I were impressed to the core, and, as with Christian looking from the other side of the river, most fervently "wished ourselves among them."

At that moment, out of a barn and through a maelstrom of bounding dogs, emerged someone I knew. She was a young woman of exceedingly good looks under the most ordinary of circumstances; but here, trimly attired in black and white, with her hair shining in the sun, she positively shone with radiance. She greeted us with warmth and graciousness—as though I were a close and valued friend, though I but vaguely knew her as a friend of my wife. Being males, Stanley glowed and I glowed, and each of us, simultaneously, became expansive and enthusiastic and rapidly vocal. I should imagine that had we been birds we should have turned cartwheels, hung upside down, and catapulted through the air, in such a frenzy of showing off were we caught up. It seemed all in the spirit of the thing. And the lady (I really believe) showed off too. She held her riding crop at an angle just a scant breath away from being grand and imperious. Her head was thrown back in laughter (at our really abominably bad light banter) with such splendor and aplomb that she had the aura of one caught in an attitude of perfection on a stage. Such moments of complete well-being and surveying of the world from a pinnacle must surely be reserved for the gods. It was all so magnificently asinine that an end must come to it, and it did—when the sparkling, effervescent lady asked us to join them in the hunt.

Stanley was obviously inextricably woven into a spider web of camera cords, light meters, lens-bearing boxes, and tripods. He is at all times well equipped for his work. But further matured, even, than his professional competence is his sense of humor. With supreme skill he instantly backed off into an impregnable professional niche, showering regret in every direction for being "previously disposed" in having to earn a living. No one could doubt his sincerity and obvious chagrin at not being able to risk his neck jumping horses over fences. But *I* (said he —with the effect of suddenly saving the day) was fortunately free of work, and he was certain of my joy and availability. And there I stood.

Still caught up in a devil-may-care attitude of deity-defying splendor, I played the Fool on a truly grand scale: when asked where I had hunted I mumbled something vague about "bush hunting in Australia." This was true enough—but there is a wide separation between poking Queensland ponies over flat saltbush and leaving the world, straight upwards, on a spirited hunter. My halfhearted plea for release centering about improper dress was short-lived; clothes, boots and all, were to be had. This, it seemed, was, in spite of our enthrallment, not a "formal" hunt but an "informal" one. There is actually not a great deal of difference to an outsider looking on; they are both "formal enough," one would say. And the principal ingredient—the horse—was easily got: "We've a barn full of 'em—all needing exercise."

And so it was that some short time later I appeared: resplendent. I wore a tweed coat and a "Rex Harrison" hat, and breeches of strong whipcord in which I resembled a movie director. My gloves were of pigskin, and I carried a cord pair to be set under a strap in the event of wet weather or slippery reins. Also, I carried a hunting crop, flayed at the end so as better to goad on a horse. I saw myself in a mirror stuck behind some bales of hay, and quailed in terror. It was as though I had been completely garbed as an aviator, taken to the airport—and then remembered that I couldn't fly. My knees shook, and I began, profusely, to perspire.

But at the same time I did some very active thinking. While Stanley was employed in a series of grand gestures before a now-swelling crowd (arranging, I thought, so that proper pictures could be had of my demise), I slipped out of a door, climbed the hill toward the main house, and, arriving there, asked a maid to show me to the library. She didn't know me—but I obviously "belonged." I went straight to the children's section (knowing the twelve-year-old daughter of the house) and found a gigantic cache—of course—of "horse books." Among them was one on *The Art and Technique of Hunting,* or some such title. I read it through completely in ten minutes with such extreme concentration that even today I can remember the tiny bug squashed on page 14. Then I went to another and scanned it with the thoroughness of a spy whose life depended on it (and I firmly believed mine did). In twenty minutes I was down the hill, into the paddock, onto my mount, and—with what I still think was the nod of a *grand seigneur*—I passed a really bemused Stanley with not so much as a quaver. I rode in company with the others to the center of a large field where I, in turn, (and in my case truly "according to the book") doffed my hat to the Master of the Hunt (but not to the Huntsmen), saluted the Whippers-in in their lovely green coats, and rode into a gaggle of acquaintances to await the start.

Now, were I telling you a story, I should be on the threshold of a climax; and I wonder what smashing kind of thing it would be. There would be a suspenseful lead-up, a lull, for gathering strength, and a thunderous scene of action culminating in loud hurrahs and throaty exclamations of Victory. At the risk of discouraging you from reading further, I must tell you it wasn't like that. There was no climax. I rode with the hunt. I took each jump in the manner prescribed by the little book—twenty-six of them. I did not fall off. I saw neither hide nor hair of a fox, and I rode back, late in the day, in a mood of quietude and sober contemplation.

My reaction as we gathered upon that hill rise, all together, waiting for the pack to strike a scent, was one—still of fear—but, also, of growing wonder. The perfection of the scene: the beauty of the horses, of the poised riders, the loveliness of the green grass and the hazy depths of the wooded hills beyond—all of it smote me like a blow. I felt the strong suppleness of the large hunter I rode sturdily set beneath me as though my own legs were four, and I could feel my own strength implanted in the earth. His ears were erect and he was taut in every fiber. I laid my hand quietly on his neck—not to pat familiarly, but as a gesture of equality; I felt only a guest, not a master. Somehow all fear left me. We waited together, he and I. Suddenly the hounds (sounding like a far-off flock of geese) changed the timbre of their tonguing. Neither horses nor riders moved. There was a blast from the hunting horn and some words made unintelligible by distance. I have seldom before or since felt quite so bow-taut, so at-the-ready, so nearly overcome with pent-up emotion. Then, at an instant only the horses really knew, there was, as one, a deep surge forward of all the mounts, forward and ever faster as though released by a spring and flying free. There was another blast from the horn, I remember, as we approached the first fence.

Well, that is that, really. I have told you all of it. But my point in doing so was this: I shall speak of it again—the hunting —for it is a part of our scene. I speak of it because it has had connotations (for me, and perhaps for you) of being a plaything of the Rich, a pose, and of little worth except as random amusement that could be found anywhere. I can tell you now that hunting is not "of and for the Rich," for I found—when later I first mingled, finally to join them—that it was not a "social" thing at all but made up of all kinds of people, bound together through mutual love, not of the horses alone, but of the *scene*. It is a *country thing*. Yes, money does enter it, as it does everything else. But your new automobile might buy three good hunting horses and the feed to keep them going for some years. It is not a matter of "exclusion of the outsiders," but that "the outsiders" refuse to look in on country things. Soon there will, no doubt, be housing developments amongst these hunting hills, and great stretches of marked-off macadam on which to park cars in front of supermarkets. But there will still be no understanding of us among the people who will come, "fleeing the city." Their daughters will ride—but it will be on motor scooters, or, who knows, personal helicopters. The horses will be gone, and the trim riders. There will be horns—but not hunting horns. There will be other things. But not for me.

The surrounding woods have been mentioned. In particular, the oak woods. Wood in the singular, however, the basic substance from which the esthetic woodland scene springs, is something far more earthbound. In a word, it wants chopping. That is, of course, if winter fires are a thing to be desired. And we think they are. Not that live trees are touched by us at any time —nor need they be. Far more dead limbs and windfalls are to be had than could possibly be used. Each winter season, with its penetrating frost, and each season of dampened earth under high winds, brings certain great trees crashing to the ground. It is a saddening sight to see the loss, for, whichever tree it might be, it has its place *there*, at that particular spot. There is a vacancy, "an empty chair" said one of the children with the snide cynicism of the young. It is true; each is missed as it goes down, and it is missed by the young as well, but it is not missed for long. There are too many. There is soon a spreading out, and the gaps are mysteriously filled.

The oaks here are principally Red oaks and Black oaks; that is, on the hills above the house. There are some White oaks, but none nearly the size of the giant Reds and Blacks. The Black oak is much the same as the Red except for its yellow-orange inner bark, the shape of its leaves (which are more indented and sharp), and the cups of its acorns which in the autumn extend halfway up the top of the nut. Also, on the eastern hill, all along its crown, there is a large stand of Chestnut oaks, the leaves of which are only slightly indented, seeming more a wide, flat, spatulate fan. Two others are found nearby, the Pin oak close down toward the salt marsh on a slope of dry land above it, and the Scarlet oak near a small bog off the main road.

Oaks have long been a heraldic symbol of staunchness and solidity. One need only take an axe to one in order to find out why. The wood is extremely hard, tough, resilient, and stringy. How many times have not my wedges flown ringing into the air when struck with the hammer rather than penetrate the oak logs. Even when split, if the wood is green, it is barely possible to keep alight. But when dried for a year or two, or if heated to a great degree by softwood kindling, the oak becomes the best and most steady of fires, giving immense heat and burning to a clean white ash.

Our fireplace seems to like oak. It burns well and does not overheat the chimney. But other woods come in from the woodpile also. Silver maple is a common one, but it burns in a ragtag manner, erratic and lackluster. Tulip poplar is a wood that throws sparks, sizzles, and explodes in gaseous abandon when wet, and so rapidly is it consumed when dry that one is perpetually forced to replenish it. Hickory burns well but is not subject to windfall. Apple is splendid, and burns with green lights. Locust is hard as iron; so is Sassafras. There is neither native spruce nor pine left standing in our woods.

It is to oak that we always return for our home fires. Each evening sees the laying of kindling, then the smaller, then the larger logs. Always do the younger children stand or kneel in silence as the moment of lighting arrives. It seems as though some deep ancestral solemnity strikes all of us at the lighting. As the flames mount and begin to roar, and as the warmth radiates and penetrates the room, and the flickering light intensifies—there seems to be a release within each of us: children chatter, backs are settled against things, laughter is introduced, and it seems as though the gods are appeased and all's well with the world. All of this has happened, just moments ago, as it has happened so many times before. Soon now, the logs will burn down to a steady, even, yellow-blue flame. Later it will turn deep orange. Still later there will be a deep ruby burning; and last of all, at bedtime, an old-rose color to the embers, still radiating heat, still even. A solid burning. Solid as is the oak.

One thing which fits neither into our oak woods nor into our marshes (but which inevitably wanders into both and gets herself lost) is our single, old Cheviot ewe. This is not "sheep country" by any stretch of license. Her presence was brought about by whim, for we were buying some hens at the Englishtown auction and suddenly there she was. Her name is Lamb Chop; but no such dire image overhangs her rotund, fleecy form. Her ostensible chore is to reduce the height of grass, but as her preference is for Number One Clover hay, which comes only in bales from the Farmers' Cooperative, our coarse grass is all but totally ignored. It is lonely for her, certainly. We must get another, perhaps. But the multiplication of mouths must be curtailed somewhere. I wonder where, however. They are all such a pleasure to us.

Our house is in the woods, as I have said. The road ends here. Down the road, for a quarter of a mile, you pass oak and laurel on the right, and some bramble, a gully, an open field beyond a holly copse, and then a tall wood of tulip poplars. At that point the little dirt road enters the main road, which in turn goes left past a clear spring and over a causeway by the salt water; to the right it goes into the nearby village, to a number of towns, cities, and to all the world—presuming that one would wish to turn to the right. Across this main road lies a large house in the distance and, in the foreground, a large barn. In front of the barn there are lawns sweeping down to the salt water. The hills lie behind. On the left stands a small group of exceedingly old and immense poplars. Over some small islands there is, in the far distance, a view over the barrier beach and out over the ocean.

In the large barn (and I have come here to tell you of it) I am fortunate to have my working quarters, located in two large rooms comprising the hayloft. The second-floor doors open out into only air, inviting trouble in the unlikely event of a speedy exit, but otherwise affording a magnificent view of the nearby water and distant seascape. The hayloft no longer holds hay but now is filled with stacks of books, working tables and furniture, and a pleasant jumble of personal effects to make it homely and livable. The road is behind the barn but little traffic comes by— the road leading to nowhere, ending in a rutted woodland path.

The woods come nearly to the back window of my eyrie, and, as I have said, the expanses of open water with their ever-changing patterns are always before me through the large loft doors (which are now of glass). There are no longer farm animals in the barn; even the hint of their former presence has now been blown away by many winters of abandonment. An orchard stands on the rise west of the barn, and nearly all of its apples are of the old-fashioned kind: a lustrous red, lightly spotted, tough skinned and tart, but having a basic sweetness and overall delectable flavor. It is—this old barn—an incomparable haven and a pleasant place in which to work.

Sitting here now reminds me, with great sadness, of my "barn squirrel." The loft has quite a low ceiling: only 7 feet high. I can easily touch it while standing. In the other parts of this quite large and commodious structure—in which, needless to say, I do not attempt to have heat—are certain crevices whereby small animals and birds can enter and, as I have, find shelter. There are skunks at the "basement" level, an occasional raccoon in the stables, barn owls (often) in the far loft, White-footed mice everywhere, and a splendid assortment of spiders, wasps, and others of their kind, each claiming his niche and "peacefully coexisting," as the (less functional but more loudly touted) modern political concept would have it. The most choice place of residence within our communal structure, however, is directly above my head in the 4-foot space above the rough ceiling, where the heat rising from my stove through the entire winter makes as toast-warm an apartment as might be desired. It is here that Gray squirrels have long made their home; usually just one, however, or sometimes two during a year. It is jealously guarded: more than once have I seen the occupant turn savagely on visiting squirrels who brashly tried to enter and lay claim.

It is natural enough, of course, that one engaged in a totally solitary work, as is mine, should quite easily form associations with wild things. "Penned up" as I am, particularly in winter, for long days on end, it is even more natural that these associations take on a greater significance than usual. No one really likes to be lonely. Certainly not I—nor do squirrels, or any other kind of animal. And, so, long associations naturally lead to conversation. Now don't misunderstand my meaning: I don't mean to indicate I have taken leave of my senses and "talk baby talk" to the poor, suffering beasts. Nor do I give insult to reason by suggesting that any but the loosest of bonds is ever formed. But bonds of a sort there have been. There is a squirrel above me now—but no rapport is there. He is new. But in years past there has been a genuine tie of sympathy on occasion between man and beast.

Three years ago I began to notice a most comic figure near the barn. It was a squirrel which, either by accident of birth or one of later date, was deprived of at least four-fifths of his tail. In fact, the remaining portion was exactly the dimensions of that less-than-satisfactory terminus found on rabbits. And the effect was remarkable, even to a veteran observer of wildlife. The casual glance bespoke a small rabbit, which, depending on your light conditions, was not necessarily gray. If in the next instant that "rabbit" should suddenly vault straight up a tree and swing from a branch, the effect was little less than startling! But as time went on I became quite used to this odd apparition, and he to me. I noticed that he would often eat the crenulated green fruits of the Osage orange trees which made a hedge between the barn and the orchard. As he gnawed at first one, then another, he would hop far more like a rabbit than a squirrel; and with his obvious preference for the large, light-green spheres, he looked for all the world like Peter Rabbit in Mr. MacGregor's cabbage patch. With the coming of winter he found the barn, and settled in above my head in the warmest section near the stove.

Since we had known each other for rather a long time by then, "conversation" began almost immediately. As I would come up the narrow stairway, followed by my old dog, I would nearly always hear a loud chatter from his nest. It was inevitably followed by a grinding of teeth and a second chittering noise. I would say "Good morning," and settle down to work. If, as it

sometimes happened, I came up and no voice greeted me, I would pause and say, more loudly than usual, "Good *morning!*" Then (as though caught napping) he would quickly chatter and grind —often giving a few extra sentences into the measure as a sort of excuse, I suppose. Many times during the long working days he would come in from the snowy outside with a particularly heavy tread and would be admonished to "Stop stamping your feet!" He would chatter loudly in answer. And upon occasion I would notice that he was long overdue in returning home, and would ask in some temper when he finally came scrabbling in, "Where in the devil have *you* been?" And always he would chatter. Once when the stove went out during the night and I failed to come in until noon, I was greeted with that which in squirrel-talk must certainly have been swearing. He grumbled all afternoon.

This rather close relationship extended over two years. During mating season and for the period of nesting he left the barn for long periods and raised a family in the tall American larch a hundred or so yards away, the only larch anywhere nearby. He had a nest obviously made of poplar leaves and (perhaps) lined with the soft, tender-green needles of the larch. Only upon occasion did he return during this period, but always, when he came, he would be as vocal and demanding as ever. Finally, in August he would "take up residence" again.

One day in November, little more than a year ago, this old friend of mine dined on apples during the greater part of the morning. I watched him carrying a whole, bright red apple, trying to go up the tree whose branches reached to the barn roof and were his principal access route home. His apple kept slipping from his teeth and falling back down to the ground. Finally, he engineered the apple over the roof; I saw him catch it once with his paws and remember thinking at the time he reminded me of a dung beetle with his ball.

At around two o'clock of the same day I was conscious of a loud report. I heard a door slam over the motor of a car, and thought vaguely of a backfire. But later in the afternoon in talking with my friend Dan, who had been trimming out brush on the west boundary, I was asked if I had seen the hunters who had been so brash as to shoot directly from their car and then to speed away like so many fugitives. I said I had not seen them but thought poorly enough of their sportsmanship, not to mention their breaking of the law. The very thought made me angry, but as I walked toward the barn I began to feel uneasy. I waited, during the afternoon, until nearly five o'clock; and then, with great relief, I heard a familiar scratching noise from the ceiling near the nest. I said, "Home at last, you scoundrel," and left my work for the day to return to the house.

For three days thereafter I heard no reaction when I spoke to the ceiling. I grew suspicious. On the fourth morning I climbed with great difficulty across the beams through the darkness to where the nest lay. He was dead, there beside his half-eaten apple. I left him untouched in his nest, and next day departed for some weeks on a business trip. When I returned I boarded up his entrance. His mummified body and the dried apple are there still.

As I have said, there is a squirrel above me yet again. He found a new entrance. But I have since moved the stove so he has not claimed the old nest. I may get to know him better. But it will never be quite the same.

November also brings us the season's last moths. It is odd, but at no other time of the year do we see the particular kind of moth which in late November visits us every year. We have never been able to find its proper name—even after consulting experts. "Experts," as you know, these days are so ultra-specialized that it is often easier to become knowledgeable oneself in a subject than to search out the proper specialist. With this problem I went to more than six "moth" people—one was a *Pyraustid* expert; another was interested in *Phalaenids;* others were knowledgeable about *Saturnidae,* the large ones, such as the Cecropia and the Luna moths—none, however, was a serious student of the "prominents," those of the Family *Notodontidae,* to which (it was easily evident by books) our moth belongs. We call it the Beech-leaf moth (though that cannot be its name). They come in numbers well after the first frosts have settled in; on very cold nights, as a great fire roars within, they are still to be seen fluttering at the panes, attracted to the light.

The "Northern lights" are called by some the *Aurora borealis.* Others call this phenomenon by other names, accompanying which are complicated theories of electron showers, light diffusion, and whatnot of scientific involvement. Here on Sandy Hook, though, our brightest aurora emanates from the tall buildings of East River Drive. If you climb to the hill's crest or walk the mile or so to the Highland cliffs, the glare of New York's skyline will subdue even the most splendid of natural displays. But from our deep little valley, looking upward into the blackness and out beyond the stars, the shifting veil of color that we call the Northern lights seems part of our woods and we lay claim to it as our own. And it is on these, now cold, nights of November that it comes.

December

The Holly Pickers

Never mind that "winter" begins on the twenty-first of December, promptly, at whatever time it is in the afternoon. Rubbish! Winter begins when it becomes miserably cold and stays that way. Winter is the most movable of Moveable Feasts. This year the cold came early; even in November it had become intense at times, and a good rain or two at 33° Fahrenheit is enough to take the spirit out of any man. However, a good snow at 31°, though infinitely more attractive, is scarcely less stimulating. Last year it remained balm and gladness far into December. Now, however, early in the month, winter has set in solidly. The children speak of "black ice" and are in a fever of digging out skates, arguing over ill-fitting wool hats, and complaining with bitter vehemence over "someone else" having lost that other glove. With complete disregard for whoever might or might not like it, winter has kicked its boots into a corner and has settled down for the period described by the gas station man, as he stopped swearing for a scant instant over the obstinacy of snow tires, as "quite a spell."

"Feeding the birds" is a universal pastime in temperate countries. Whether in Russia, Scandinavia, England, Japan, or the

39

United States (or turned about: Argentina, South Africa, or Australia), the birds are fed. It is quite a business. Sunflower seeds, peanut hearts, and millet are piled by the hundreds of tons in warehouses to be channelled out to "bird lovers," i.e., you and me. Birds have become expensive, as you have learned. But nearly everyone feels they are worth it all. The feeding goes on year by year. Even the "tray" arrangement is a rather universal thing. There are often balls of suet, scrambled egg, peanut butter, and other enticements in addition, but usually seeds and crumbs make up the fare wherever one may be.

When we lived in Australia we were directly on the sea in Queensland but still birds came in profusion. The Mudlark and Black-backed magpie would patrol the grass; Lorikeets and Cockatiels would wheel by; Kookaburras sat on the fringes, and doves were everywhere. In England, the winter tray will be filled with Bramblings, Chaffinches, the robin (the English robin), blackbird (a thrush), Song thrush, the House sparrow (our "English" sparrow), nuthatches, and the Blue tit, Coal tit, and others. And here in New Jersey we have our "regulars": first of all come the chickadees and Tufted titmice (both tits, similar to the English ones); then a scattering of finches—the Song, Field, Tree, Fox, and White-throated sparrows; the Juncos, Purple finches, and Pine siskins; Blue jays come too frequently, scattering everything with their raucous behavior; Cardinals are frequent, and both the Downy and Hairy woodpeckers and White-breasted nuthatches are constantly seeking the suet cage.

Infrequently there will be Evening grosbeaks and a very occasional crossbill. In recent years the Mockingbird has come in upon occasion. Brown creepers lace their way up and down the trees nearby, and nearly always a Myrtle warbler remains throughout the winter and flutters near the windows hoping for an occasional insect hiding in a crevice. Perhaps because we are so far from town, seldom do we see even an individual English sparrow and few Starlings come near our tray. All in all, it is a pleasant, conversational—even garrulous—assemblage. Somehow our feeding of the birds (and the birds feeding back of companionship to us) makes winter less of a sterile and bitter thing. There is so much happiness in a handful of seeds.

Somehow it has all happened in a hurry. I mean this business of winter. It seems that only days ago I was lying at full length in the scented, warm leaves, considering the hot bright sun and the amplitude of the perfection around me. Now I have just come in from having slipped in the wet snow while carrying a towering armload of logs. The logs were not at all incommoded, but I am sore and bruised and wet.

Before I went down like a poled ox into the snow, I had taken a half hour to range round the woods and into the swamp for a look at what Ernest Thompson Seton's Yan (a friend of mine for so long a time I cannot remember when I didn't know him) called "the mud albums." Described in another way: "animal tracks." But my albums, this day, were of snow. Last night's wet snow was over a base coating of a previous inch. The step of any foot, large or small, into this virginal blanket is recorded with stark clarity, like that of a cat who has walked first into soot and then across a clean sheet. No one abroad after the snowfall escaped having his pedal message clearly read.

The first markings I noticed were those of the small birds that had flown down to find seeds near the door. There were not many, for the feeding tray drew them like a magnet. Then I noticed that a White-footed mouse had come out from under a tangle of small holly bushes to sample the birds' sunflower seeds. There seemed to be only one mouse, but a number of trips. His tail dragged at each hop. Since I was up and outside before the chickens and ducks were let out, there was no doubt that a crow had been fossicking for a stray kernel of corn. And his mark was aerial as well, for he had flown from the ground and pounced on a low dogwood branch, leaving his footprints and brushing the snow from the outer branches. He was sloppier even than that, for he had left a wing mark and had overturned a small pan with his beak. The pan left a round disk of bare earth and brown grass. A Blue jay had also plummeted down for corn; his broad wing primaries marked the spot.

As I walked from the yard there were Cottontail rabbit and more White-footed mouse tracks everywhere, a veritable criss-cross. Further on, there was the steady fore-and-aft tread of a fox. The fox twice smelt the rabbit tracks and once pawed the entrance to a mouse tunnel. Further still, in the marshy area by the stream, I saw a small "lift" to the snow in an irregular pattern, as though a garden hose had been placed under a sheet. On the top of this tiny ridge at one point was an air hole where a small nose had been run up through the snow. It was the trail of a Short-tailed shrew, that diminutive but powerful molelike creature with small fear and large appetite. Very unlike a mole is he, with "mouselike" feet, a Cyrano-snout, and multiple, sharp teeth. He has a poisonous secretion in the back of his mouth, numerous cousins—and, for all I know, a fat and lethargic wife . . . at any rate, it was the trail of a Short-tailed shrew: *Blarina*

brevicauda, which means short-tailed, which he is. Yet further on, a Gray squirrel had gone *pa-lunk, pa-lunk* between two trees—this not being the noise he made, for I didn't hear or see him; but his tracks were exactly four, consisting of two footprints side by side. He had jumped from a tree trunk, taken two leaps, and had gone up another trunk without (it seemed) coming down again. There appeared to be a knothole toward the top of the second tree, but who knows—they jump like the wind from branch to branch.

And that was all I saw. I left the hillside to which my own erratic path led, and returned home. The fowls had been loosed since I had gone out, and the yard looked as though an army of ducks, chickens, geese, cross-eyed bandicoots, and Hairy Ainus, all raving mad, had been staging an earnest custard-pie fight: there was spilled grain, overturned water pans, a trail of laying mash, and a disgusting scatter of straw. It looked as though someone with manic intent had wildly set about to destroy a book. The pages of my "snow album" were in a ruin. It was then that I gathered up the firewood and glissaded into a heap at the front door.

The tidal flats in winter are as bleak as any tundra. If there is a snowstorm at a time of low tide, it seems as though many acres more of land are suddenly risen from the sea. The flood tide, however, soon sets the crooked arithmetic straight. And when ice forms at high tide on the small islands covered with marsh grasses, the ice breaks in jagged edges at the ebb, leaving a ridiculous fringe 3 feet in the air, like a tutu on an elephant.

The gulls remain with us during the winter and sail on buoyant wings over the frozen tidal flats with as little care as though it were midsummer. The Herring gull is here, the Ring-billed, and the Great Black-backed gull; all here in the deadest part of winter. They sit on the edges of the ice or patrol the tide edge, combing and recombing the flotsam for something of a gustatory nature. Near the shore there will be muskrat tracks. There are ducks, both "paddle" ducks (Mallards, Blacks, Widgeon, and the like) and "bay" ducks (Canvasback, Scaup, and their kind). The "sea" ducks (Scoters, Old Squaw, etc.) seldom come inside until late in the season.

Few ducks of any kind, however, are in constant residence during this season, for this month is the height of the legal hunting season and from dawn until dusk (and illegally, after dusk) there is a constant staccato barking of guns. Hunters pole or paddle their low duck boats among the sedge islands or build blinds along the shore wherever permissions can be obtained. Permissions are rarely granted in our cove, however; thus there is a constant putting-off and chastisement, called "just deserts" by the residents and "harassment" by the hunters. Who is right? Each, in his own way. Enlightened legislation and enforcement for the mutual good is essential. The private owner must be assured of his privacy; but also, the hunter must be given access to certain lands and waters—and those lands must be large enough and ecologically secure enough to permit natural renewal of loss. Even now, through his support of wildlife management legislation as well as compliance with game laws, the hunter replenishes what he takes. But if unbridled private enterprise is allowed to contaminate, pollute, and destroy cover; to be allowed loopholes in zoning laws, to fill in and to obliterate wetlands, and to amoebically encircle and engulf these tracts of ecologically sound land, nothing will remain. The private owner will be surrounded by a sterile wasteland, and the hunter (who is the embodiment of man asserting his virility) will be drawn to the effeminancy of the nihilistic pursuits which, even now, threaten his interests and subvert all natural law.

Duck hunting, then, is a tenuous survivor in this estuary of ours. The shooting of ducks goes on—but none will deny it is not like "the good old days." The area is still very wild in spots —as I have described to you—but in others it is built up to such a degree that neither hunting nor any other wild pursuit will ever be possible again. Is it too widely divergent from reality to hope that a coexistence of interests is yet possible? I hold that it *is* possible and there *is* hope.

Returning from the tidal flats, I met two duck hunters on the causeway, their guns broken in a proper manner and their licenses in full display in the middle of their backs. They had seen no ducks and were disconsolate. One of them was quite wet, having fallen into the water; and the other, though dry, was shivering with the cold. He said he was wearing electrically heated underwear and that the contraption had had a short circuit. I invited them into the barn to get warm and we talked of ducks for two hours.

Yesterday I came to the barn the "long way" round the field instead of the road, and saw mink tracks for the first time in a number of years. The snow is gone now; the tracks were in mud at the edge of the salt marsh. It is just possible that I was mistaken, for they were considerably overlaid with tracks of raccoons and possums, both of which, presumably, were there at low tide paddling around after mollusks. If it was a mink (and I believe it was) it will be a newcomer, for the one I knew some years ago was taken by a trapper. I can well give thought now to the welfare of my hens, for one mink will go through a hen house like a ball through tenpins. Not that they make a regular thing of it, but once they take the notion they are as ferocious as one can imagine.

A mink is a curious beast. Low-slung, more supple than a cat, they have almost a reptilian way about them. Of course, weasels, skunks, otters, martens, fishers—even the wolverine— are all in the same family as the mink; or, rather, they are all "weasels": the Family *Mustelidae*. They are blood-lusting carnivores, quick, powerful, and aggressive. All have some sort of pungent musk gland, the skunk being the worst to some people —but to me, a "good, rich mink" (and here I do not speak of coloration) is enough to stop my breathing. The fur of nearly all of these animals is well known in a commercial way, being lustrous and fine of texture, but also strong as well. This kind of animal is becoming rare here now, except for the skunk— which is to the mink as a garbage scow is to a destroyer. The otter is long since gone and the mink is scarce. The small weasel, still, is occasional. He will come and go. But we see few of his kind at any time. The presence of a mink is not particularly desirable. But, then, neither is the complete vacuity of his absence.

Tracks of mink in the snow are suggestive of wilderness. But any such inference related to this region as a whole would be ludicrous. It is true that our little "pocket" is a small, vestigial remainder of wilderness, but changes are being wrought everywhere and at a furious pace. Everything has changed since we came here.

In fact, it has changed to such a degree that perhaps it is as well some of the old-timers we've known didn't live to see it. I speak of the old trolley conductor I knew; of Charlie, who ran the gas station in town. The old ones are mostly gone now. Now there is no trolley. There is a bus. And it lumbers along in a cloud of noxious fumes. The new man at the gas station has taken down the faded needlepoint in the old frame that said: "Travel east, Travel west/ After all, Home's best," which may have been dreadful, but was anyhow different from the gaudy calendar advertising gaskets that has a color photograph of a fleshy, brown-haired woman whose clothes peel off with a greasy piece of acetate, revealing her naked, her great breasts pneumatically askew. And the same man has put up great strings of cheap and tawdry pennants which flap inanely, signifying nothing. I have stopped going there. Now I drive across the river to a great, antiseptic, neon-lighted gas emporium where they give away stamps and dishes and cannot understand why I keep giving them back.

These neon oases are a product of an age. Our age. So are the shopping centers—these huge blobs of parking area with their sleazy, eye-searing signs on squared-off, ammonia-smelling brick cubicles—like a burned flapjack crowned with a pat of greasy margarine. These dispensers of cheap drugs, cheap shoes, cheap food, and whatever else they sell, have also cheap canaries:

"Cheep! Cheep! Cheap! Cheap!" they are advertised. And the lovely golden things, one atop the other in light green plastic prisons, sing their hearts out under signs reading "Buy me, Bub —$1.98."

Where there were apple and peach orchards, a few miles away, there are now row on row of houses. Beyond these there is a gap of trees, left standing because of a small stream. The stream is filled with bicycle tires, rusted oil cans, and filth. The water is a light gray, and the rocks have a fringe of hydra-like scum clinging to them. And then there are further rows of houses behind which, across a burning dump, are more houses. There are kitchen middens along the shore where Indians used to come with clams. The clams now, in all the region washed by the Raritan basin, are polluted. This world that is different from ours is just five miles from our little village with its one store and minute post office; five miles to its heart, that is—its tentacles reach out further. And with each year they come closer. There is a new concrete foundation near the Stone Church. The trees were ploughed down by a bulldozer and scraped into a great pile to be burned; but they were only partly burned, for they still lie like jackstraws, charred and broken, their limbs covered with caked mud and ashes.

Thank Heaven, it has snowed at last! A proper snow—not the heavy, wet kind we have had so far that has fallen and melted, fallen again and melted again. I do not mean that I revel in the stuff. I have grown to an age when it is less than pleasant to contemplate. But I do not suggest there is anything wrong with snow. I know it is I who have changed. My rejoicing over its arrival is simply relief at being free of the Damoclean sword of its perpetual threatening.

How I do grumble about it as it falls! As it continues to descend at night, in fine flakes, and to blow in little drifts against the porch railing, I go out from time to time to "see if it is snowing"—knowing full well it is. I watch its soft descent in the circle of light from the porch, as a cat watches the fall of a dandelion wisp. And I come back in, stamping and mumbling, asserting that it is a damned nuisance, but delight in feeling its cool touch on my face. My hair is covered with tiny drops as I come back into the warmth of the firelit room. My wife responds to my cantankerous humor by silently handing me—without looking up from her book—a copy of a collected Robert Frost, opened to "Stopping by Woods on a Snowy Evening." Sitting before the fire, I read on to "Dust of Snow" . . . I read "In the Home Stretch," because I always do . . . and with "Good Hours" I linger, reading it slowly over, once again.

I rise to poke the fire, and then quietly go to the door and open it again for the seventh time in an hour.

Female patience having been stretched too far, I am asked rather sharply, "Will you please stop forever opening that door?"

"It is lovely, isn't it?" I answer.

Today we are snowed in. It has not quite ended; there are still those few small flakes coming down. But perhaps they are being blown from the trees. The sky is gray. As gray as a hornet's nest. Being snowed in is pleasant. That is, for the first few hours. The snow is unbelievably deep after the scant 4 inches I saw last night. It is soft, like fine powder. It is being gently blown in little, lazy whirlwinds a few inches in width, and is drifted and corniced and every way like (looking down) the wastelands of the Arctic must look from a few miles height. The snow is completely unviolated; not a speck or depression or any imperfection mars its surface. It is complete. There is no bird call. No sound.

Moments later there is a sudden cry that somewhat resembles joy in an irrepressible state (or mortal agony, or whatever it is), quickly muffled in snow and a slamming door, and a small boy is seen floundering like a porpoise in an element entirely in keeping with his nature. Above the admonitions from the kitchen about the inadvisability of slamming doors, and queries about whether or not gloves have been worn, galoshes buckled, and hat pulled over the ears, I hear even greater howls of delight as the small force sees the chickens are still unattended and swims off—to torture them, I suppose. As I look out the window it seems impossible that so much devastation to any element or to any thing could be achieved in so short a time. The lovely, gentle blanket of soft snow is a contorted ruin. There are deep plowlike furrows in every imaginable direction, like wood beetle tracks under cedar bark. There is also one small glove, half buried. The hens are reprieved from the dreadful fate of each being hauled out by a leg to "see the snow" as dire threats enforce a retreat to pick up the lost glove—at about which time there is the aroma of pancakes and sausages coming from the kitchen.

About an hour later I am informed that "someone" (never himself) left the snow shovel outside—"somewhere," it is added (meant to denote complete impossibility of recovery). Soon there are four reluctant children up to their thighs ploughing in a line to exhume the shovel. After it becomes clear that this procedure will not be called off until successful, the shovel is somehow magically "found." Soon it is being put to use. A caterpillar of path wanders drunkenly toward the place where the road, *ante nivis,* had been known to lie.

During the late afternoon the road plough finally comes. Being at the dead end of a dirt lane deep in the woods, it is inevitable that we should be last to be dug out—especially when the electric wires are down. This time, thank Heaven, they have remained intact.

Christmas began with St. Lucia's Day, the Scandinavian "Festival of Lights" celebrating the passing of the ebb in the year's descent into night. It hasn't a thing to do with Christmas, being pagan. But Christian (an adjective here) love is encompassing enough to support a little good, honest paganism; as it is to permit our *pepparkarkor* cookies to be made in the form of the Star of David.

"Christmas in the woods"—two days ago—brought the birthday of Jesus Christ, the birthday of our daughter, a seeming half-ton of assorted paraphernalia to be stepped over for days, friends, eggnog, food, song, sweetness, warmth, and light. I am infinitely happy it is over. No good thing should be made to last too long. But wrenching away the effects of Christmas is, in all the year, the one impossible thing; only will Twelfth Night bring an end.

Christmas cheer and Christmas love are one thing, however. Christmas thieves are another. Our woods are interspersed with trees known as the American holly. It is native, of these parts from "time immemorial" (whatever in Heaven that is! I like things to be specific). It has not the splendid, glossy, dark green of the English holly, but it is good enough, green enough, and covered with red berries enough, to be viewed as a thing of beauty. Unfortunately, it is viewed not only by us but by other people also, as a thing of beauty. And things of beauty are not often to be had in these times without the exchange of money. But our woods are "free," people joyfully decide, and holly is "only a tree." And so they come, to strip great limbs of it and to smash the branches and scarify the bark. They bring ropes, that they will be able to climb for mistletoe. Not one believes he is "stealing." It is all in the Spirit of Christmas that such bounty is given—"bounty," as it was once wrathfully shouted at me from a carefully considered distance, "given by the Almighty Hand of Jesus Christ!" I could not have agreed more, and I give thanks with all my being. It is all in the Spirit of Christmas, then, that they are all thrown out on their heads.

Some few days after Christmas there was a sudden thaw. The snow became the consistency of Italian ice; as wet and as completely soggy as the solid state can be without becoming liquid. It is not plastic enough, even, to form into a ball. It merely squeezes out through the fingers in supersaturate messiness and splashes up at you from the ground.

I am back at work again in the barn. The walk between house and barn is no longer pleasant. The thaw has caused an upheaval of the ground. The summer charm of being on a dirt road is dampeningly dissipated by the turning of dirt into mud —as the sweetness of cream turns into sour curds. There is still snow, particularly in the areas of drift. But it is all seen to be sinking into the ground, as one might imagine a ship at sea, slowly, irretrievably sinking downward into oblivion.

There are no birds. Not even at the feeding tray at home. The wet ground under the big spruce by the south window is covered with uneaten seeds. I did hear a chickadee this morning. And there—just now—is a disconsolate crow. Practically nothing by way of wildlife is abroad. Can you imagine the soft, downy fur of a Cottontail rabbit? And can you imagine him, soaked to the skin, in this wringing-wet woods filled with sodden mud and melting snow? So can he . . . so he is safe and warm in his dry burrow under some stump. And can you imagine a fox, silken-haired and softly bushy-tailed? I saw one once—a Red fox—who had slipped on some moss while crossing a log over the gully stream. He had not only fallen into the water but had ploughed through an expanse of soft, black mud in order to get to the bank. He was a sight! His lovely soft coat was plastered to his body, his splendid brush was flattened like a folded umbrella, and his legs and belly were glued with the viscous mud—but, worst of all, his head had survived unscathed, and, in all its four-pointed Reynardness, looked full-blown and glorious, as one might imagine a house cat with the mumps! And so, there is very little to be seen. There is a dead Woolly bear caterpillar being washed down the road in a runnel of melted snow. Perhaps he told a lie.

Tomorrow, there will be a new year. But before this one ends (perhaps as a sort of penance) I write out of compassion for a spider. Can you understand that? No, of course you cannot. It is, I suppose, simply an adjunct of great weariness which sets me off to write an epitaph for a spider.

But I do not think it such a foolish thing. I had come to know her (I can safely say "her," I believe; it is usually so with spiders). She was a large Wolf spider, a jumping, hunting sort. Noting that it was unusually late in the season for spiders, I had seen her round my study, just in, out, or at the corner of things, quietly going about, generally minding her business.

Today, the last day of December, was gray and chill with much rain and considerable damp. The heater was working but was turned low. It was chill enough in the barn that, when I reached under the lamp for a pencil, I noticed the pleasant warmth from the small circle of light. So did the spider. At some time when I had my eyes averted she walked (not "crept" —this rather noble sort of spider steps out most firmly) into the corner of lamp-glow and stretched out—yes, stretched out —and took in the warmth. Being busy, I spoke to her, saying something about "room enough for two"—but had cause to return immediately to my work.

Some time later I stopped work and, sitting back in my chair, just missed braining her with a pencil which, rolling heavily on its six sides, came to rest only a scant inch from her. Quite un-daunted, she moved but a fraction, eyed the "tree trunk" somewhat suspiciously, and rather languidly (I thought) sent out one of her eight legs to casually explore the object. Satisfied, she set about to enjoy her comfort in a way I had never thought of spiders doing: she stretched one leg and then another, in quite a satisfied way, as though every fiber of her being felt the beneficence of that stretching. She crossed two of her hind legs; why, I cannot say, but it was a most casual gesture. One could almost feel an extension of her pleasure as she drank deeply of the warmth.

I went on for two hours, intermittently writing, getting up to find books, taking the dog to walk. She was there all that time, having turned a little, perhaps to assume a more comfortable position. Undoubtedly she slept. I tapped with a pencil point near her head. She only idly scratched with a foot in response.

After a few hours I forgot her presence under the annoyance of having lost a reference. It simply could not be found and I grew to be very tired. The rain was increasing and the outside gloom seemed to penetrate the window glass. Turning from the window in no mood of pleasure, I saw a rather large and furtive shadow streak under some crumpled papers. Vaguely thinking of the amazingly persistent *Polistes* (a kind of wasp), which sometimes at this time of the year is awakened by the heat and stupidly crawls about my barn room carrying an often unjustly used sting, I impatiently stamped on the paper. With my foot yet on it, I felt a sudden pang of doubt and regret for my lack of charity toward whatever it was under my foot. I looked with anxiety toward the circle of warm lamplight on my table. It was empty. I raised my foot and slowly unfolded the paper. There she lay dead, her poor body crumpled up and the paper soiled with her body juices; just a cold stain. I wrapped her in her paper shroud and, somehow seeking reparation in a too-late gentleness, I placed her in the wastebasket. Then, calling to my dog—who, being old, had slept unknowingly through the drama —I went out into the dampness and dark and walked toward the house in the rain.

January

Time of Displacement

Tonight our yard was filled with ducks. That would not seem strange, since in amidst assorted fowls we keep, as you have learned, ducks of the barnyard variety. But these ducks were not our ducks. They were diving ducks—of a kind called Greater Scaup—and they had as much place in our oak woods as would a giraffe.

There is, and has been, a dense, low-lying fog. The lightship horn has been sounding all day and night until, now, even she seems hoarse. We had had a quiet evening, and I was attending to that most ancient of nocturnal rites which has always (it would appear) fallen to be Man's lot: "putting out the dog." Moments after the dog was off into the Stygian gloom with a bound, there was a kind of explosion: a tremendous beating of wings, frenzied bleatings, excessive turmoil—the dog, not barking, but most vigorously "laying to"—and I (now) laying to at the dog. As I collared the dog there was, abruptly, almost as if at a signal, complete silence.

I was very angry indeed with the dog and gave her a firm lick or two. "Getting into the ducks" passes for a major canine offense. Having bellowed for a light, a light was brought. What the light disclosed was a good number of the kinds of ducks I have mentioned, all quite confused and running and falling and blundering away into the darkness. It would sound better to be able to say "the air was filled with a blizzard of feathers" —but the air was not at all; first, because these ducks have a sort of armor plate of feathers, not a billowy mass of down, and secondly, the dog was probably quite as frightened as were they.

Quiet restored, we got down to facts. What had happened, of course, was that a wedge had flown too low in the fog, hit the trees (here quite high), and had cascaded down. Being sea ducks—or, rather, "bay" ducks—they had not the means, as would ordinary wild ducks (such as the Mallard or Pintail), of rising straight upward and beating off to seaward. These ducks are unable to take off into the air from land; they must, by means of ever-increasing foot-pushings of water, slowly gain altitude over a level and liquid runway, much after the fashion of a heavily loaded airplane. It is by no means that they are aerodynamically unsound; they are beautiful and arrow-like when airborne—but until they are in the air, or can bob upon the water, they are at an ungainly disadvantage. And so they made a pitiful display in their attempts to escape.

That is why we shall never know their number or how many went to the foxes or met some other unpleasant end. Since our presence could only do them injury, we rid ourselves of the dog, switched off the light, and quietly listened in the silent darkness. When all seemed more composed we again turned on the flashlight and, one by one, began seeking them out. Now quite calm, blinded by the light, they docilely permitted themselves to be picked up. So docile indeed were they that they seemed like pliable rubber ducks. They simply lay back so we could stroke them or manipulate their wings or legs. Their lovely, brilliant yellow eyes shone like gems on the dark green velvet that was their heads. Their broad bills were a soft, pale blue (they are often popularly known as either Bluebills or Broadbills). I could see, by spreading a wing, the long central expanse of white which is a field mark in separating the Greater from their cousins the Lesser Scaup.

When we had gathered up all we could find—numbering about a half-dozen—we took them all into the car and ferried them to the causeway at the bottom of the road. Several splashes and it was done: back in water, back home. They made no sound, but bobbed to the surface and quickly swam out of the fog-dimmed circle of the car's lights.

The next day I found a female Scaup (ours were all males, by the way) dead on the road on the main street of the nearby village. There were lines of telephone wires directly overhead and her neck was broken. I wondered about the number of other such tragedies which probably occurred under the canopy of that enveloping fog.

January got off to a splendid start. The thaw continued until the night of the fourth. Then it suddenly became bitterly cold. The wind howled out of the northwest as though blown down a great pipe from the Arctic. For two days it neither moved a degree from its course nor did it abate as much as a fraction in intensity. Then it abruptly stopped. It was eerily calm, but the intense cold continued. Twigs snapped as tiny pockets of moisture were swollen under the pressure of the ice that formed. And twice there were loud reports, as of gunfire, as trees or large branches reacted similarly to the cold. The stars were brilliant in a sky which seemed to have settled close to the earth. Orion—the hunter, my favorite among constellations—sparkled with an icy blue light. The cold was neither penetrating nor particularly unpleasant, just dry, and quietly numbing.

Now the cold has broken. The weather remains clear but a south wind has come up and the temperature has risen to nearly 24°. It seems almost tropical in comparison. I walked down from the barn at noon to watch the ducks.

For some reason, as I approached the high bank overlooking the sedge islands and the barrier beach, I failed to notice any ducks whatever. Perhaps it was because I was looking downward and wondering how grass could ever come back again, green and luxuriant, after such a pummelling as it was receiving during winter's ravaging months. Or perhaps I was musing about the condition of the ancient mulberry tree whose major limb seemed in danger of breaking. One of these things, surely, for I remember thinking hard on each. At any rate, it seems I had not looked up, for had I done so I would have seen them: two female Old Squaws just over the lip of the bank—on (of all things) dry land! It was a question as to which of us was the more surprised. They both fell—they made no attempt to fly— the forty-odd-foot drop to the water, and raced, panic-stricken over the water and into the air and away.

Old Squaws are a sea duck—here, at least. It is unusual for us to see them on land of any kind. It is for that reason that I was astonished to see the two birds at such an elevation.

Why the name Old Squaw? I thought I'd a notion—but I looked it up in one of the principal authorities on the subject.* This is what it said:

> COLLOQUIAL NAMES IN LOCAL USE: Callithumpian duck, refers to the birds' varied notes (improvised bands of uncertain musical ability are called callithumpian bands); caccawee (also spelled cockawee, kakawi, and in other ways); granny, ha-ha-way (Cree Indian name from the note, as are so many of the name of this species); hell's chicken; hound; jack-owly; jay-eye-see; kla-how-yah (Indian name); knock-molly; longtail; longtailed duck; mammy duck; mommy; o-i; old billy (males); old granny; old injun (males); old-mammy; old-molly; old-wife (sometimes written alewife or contracted to ol-wye— the term o-i, above, probably is an extreme shortening of old wife); organ duck; pintail; quandy; scoldenore; scolder; singing duck; siwash; son-son-sally duck; south-southerly (a name much varied as s'other, southerland, southerly, south-south-southerly, etc.); squaw, swallow-tailed duck; teet; Uncle Dick, winter duck.

A surfeit? And those were only the "common" names. Its scientific name is *Clangula hiemalis,* meaning a "noisy winter

---

* *The Ducks, Geese and Swans of North America,* by F. H. Kortright, The American Wildlife Institute, 1943.

duck." This is one instance, perhaps, that you might well prefer the Latin. "Uncle Dick"? Ah, well, everyone to his choice.

Thus being able to tell you nothing of the duck's name myself, I feel at something of loose ends in going further. That is, I am no duck expert, and I cannot speak Cree. "Jay-eye-see," "kla-how-yah," and "ha-ha-way" mean not a thing to me. I shall draw you a little picture instead, which you will find (hopefully right side up) somewhere off in a margin. Like *that,* you see; with a long tail. Well, it is a pretty thing, the Old Squaw; particularly the male (which is usually the case among ducks). Such widely divergent and such equally beautiful patterns of coloration in summer and winter plumage are most infrequently found. The colors are soft sepias and umbers, adjacent to white, which, in winter, is sometimes tinged with a pale pink on the head. The eyes are variable, but generally on the lighter side, as a light hazel or straw color. And the feet are bluish gray. Altogether it is an exceptionally attractive duck. As you can see, the male has a long tail, the female has not. Most

of us see Old Squaws only in winter. I have seen them in their summer dress in Alaska, however. But I was so used to them at home, here, they looked odd to me in their summer plumage. They nest only in the tundra regions of the far north.

Here we see the Old Squaw mainly from the beach strip. They float in little groups and are the quickest to dive of any ducks I know. Their movements are swift and, in flight, they fly irregularly and twist and turn in formation, showing one side, then the other—light to dark and back again—as do certain shore birds. Upon occasion (as you have seen) they will come to our cove. But not often. Generally we can find them, well enough, but one has to go into the sea to do it.

Their voice is quite remarkably variant in scale and pitch. They "babble." It is a voice high-pitched and fluted, and they seem to talk all the time. It is said that their windpipe has a coiled arrangement, and an additional "voice-box" with a lightly stretched membrane on one side to increase the volume of sound, much like the Manncode bird of paradise. The sound of this latter bird is a resonant and loud call, easily audible two miles away. The Old Squaw, too, can be heard at a great distance. For greater clarity I leave you again with the experts as to the exact nature of their call: "Ow-owly, owly, owly; ow-ow-owdle-ow; ah, ah, ah, ong, ong-onk; a-leedle-a, a-leedle-a, ar-hi-look." There. Remember that it was not I who spoke with such authority. I know very little of such things.

I do know that the sea ducks are among my favorites. The Old Squaw, the Golden-eyes (there are two), and the Scoters (three) comprise for me the "sea ducks." The more hyperborean Eiders do occasionally come down this far in winter, but I have not seen one south of Rhode Island. There are others, surely, found at sea, but these I prefer to call the "bay ducks": the Canvasback, Redhead, Greater and Lesser Scaup, the Bufflehead, Ruddy duck, Ring-necked duck, and the Mergansers (there are three). Of course, you may find any and each of these giving the lie to my categorizing by being found quite far from any salt water, sitting on some inland reservoir. But generally my breakdown holds true. This is the way we find it here, at any rate.

While I am on the subject, a third category are the inland ducks, often called "paddle ducks" for they tip up their tails and feed on the bottom of shallow ponds; they are not "diving" ducks, as are all those previously mentioned. Among this group are: the Mallard, the Black duck, the Baldpate (or Widgeon; a European Widgeon is not overly rare in North America, also), the Gadwall, the Pintail, the Blue and Green-winged Teals, the Shoveller, and the Wood duck. Only the last two are in any great way different from the true "paddle ducks." The Shoveller has a broad, spatulate bill with which it is even more adept at bottom feeding than the others, having more complicated straining lamellae, the bristlelike projections on the bill's inner sides. Also it has a more elongated intestine, employed in the digestion of the minute grasses and organisms found in the muddy ooze in which it feeds. And the Wood duck is essentially a "tree" duck, nesting in trees and flying often to quite solid ground to feed. Each of these last, however, is commonly found in the company of any of the others in its general group. Few of these ducks are ordinarily in the open sea (least of all the Wood duck)—but as sea ducks are blown landward in storms, such ducks as these are as often blown seaward. So any of a number of strange admixtures of situations can be brought about under certain conditions.

I have gone on only so that, in one (hopefully purgative) dose, I can quickly set things aright by way of a roster. I shall perhaps again mention certain of these ducks, so that the compilation of even a roughly categorized list may be of some use. But I began—and I should like to finish—with the "sea" ducks.

The Golden-eyes or Whistlers are alternately called by both names, since it is difficult to ascertain which is the more appropriate. Their eyes are so brilliantly golden that—until you hear their wings whistle in flight—you are certain in your own mind.

The whistling wings will change you. And then you will have doubts—and, in a word, will probably end up like everyone else: using both names interchangeably.

They are very bouncy and happy-go-lucky ducks, the Whistlers (Golden-eyes). The "American" has a broad, rounded, white spot on his cheek, while the Barrow's has one shaped more like a crescent; the first also has, generally, a dark, greenish head, while the latter's is usually of a more purple cast. They are a diving duck, living on mollusks, crustaceans, and the like, as a rule. They nest in the north, but not in the tundra; for they have the odd quirk of being a "tree duck" at nesting time, the young literally being made to jump to the ground from the nesting hole. Here in coastal New Jersey the Golden-eye (Whistler) seems to come into bays and brackish water more readily than do the Old Squaw and Scoters.

The Scoters have always interested me. They are dark birds for the most part; that is, their bodies and wings are mostly black. All three American varieties have a swelling on the bill which resembles the often-domesticated Muscovy duck. The White-winged Scoter is the more common, and the easiest to identify by its white secondary wing feathers. The leading one-third of the bill has a red marking. The Surf Scoter is possibly equal in numbers to the White-winged. It is identified by a total lack of white on any part but its head, on which the male has a white spot both fore and aft. The bill is multicolored in orange, red, and white. And in the American Scoter the male is entirely black but for a bulbous yellow protuberance behind its nostril. The females of all three species are an overall dusky brown, with inconsequential white cheek patches. I think my liking of Scoters stems from their proximity to the sea, with its smell of salt and invigorating clarity. The White-winged and Surf Scoters often are found inland, but the (more rare) American Scoter is seldom found away from the ocean itself. They all have a flight that is singularly undramatic except that they fly in great irregular strings, low over the water. Ninety per cent of their food is mollusks or other sea animals.

Scoters are called "coots" in New England (a highly inaccurate term, as there is an entirely different bird of the rail family that already possesses the name). Although they are shot with regularity—for they come readily to decoys—the flesh is generally considered to be less than satisfactory. One recipe is reported to run: "Take one Scoter and nail it to a board. Put the board in the sun for a week. Then carefully remove the bird from the board, throw away the bird, and eat the board."

The "bay" ducks are divers also. Our cove is filled with many different species during January and February. The flights of bay ducks finally becomes a most obvious part of the littoral scene. At one time or the other I have seen every kind in all three categories either in our own estuary or within close sight of it—that is, just over the beach strand. Our waters are still reasonably clean, being flushed twice daily by a strong tide from the sea, but they are becoming dirtier every year with the increasing use of motor boats. Fortunately, the ducks and motor

boats do not coincide. The last of the thousands of waterfowl are well up, out, and away before the first of the boats is launched for the season.

At just about this date last year, the telephone rang (no seismic occurrence, surely, but it had some considerable repercussions). It was someone I knew connected with the oceanographic laboratory at Sandy Hook.

"We've got a baby seal down here that's hurt. You're a mammalogist. Aren't seals in your department?"

I cautiously allowed they were.

He went on to ask, "What do I do?"—knowing full well that I would end up doing it.

I, again with caution, asked, "Are you certain it's a *baby* seal? That sounds very strange."

"Oh yes, just a baby!" he promised.

I asked what kind of seal. He didn't know.

All the way down in the car I suspected exactly the kind of put-up job this would be. Had the call come from the head of the laboratory, Dr. Lionel Walford, a veteran scientist and well-known authority on marine life, I should not have felt so ill at ease, for I would have been given exact information.

My arrival, on one of the most frigid and bitter nights of that year, was heralded with: "He's so helpless" (running for his coat) "and sick" (taking another swig of coffee) "and you'll take to him right away" (putting on his hat, pulling me through the door, and dropping me next to the parking lot).

There, on the cold steel floor of a pickup truck, was the "baby." She (first of all, a female) was fully grown and weighed well over a hundred pounds. She was a Harbor seal, *Phoca vitulina*. She was injured, with a ghastly propeller slash (or so I suspected) on her flank. And she was soaking wet, exposed to a cutting, vicious wind in a temperature of something like 15° above zero. Also, she was wallowing in a combination of sea water, urine, and her own blood, and was frightened half to death. Besides, she had a rasping cough and considerable lung congestion. I was furious about the poor animal's condition, but it was hardly anyone's fault; the research vessel had found her, unable to move, wedged into some rocks. I went in to the telephone and put in a call to Dr. Carleton Ray at the new aquarium on Long Island. He listened to the situation and said, yes, he'd like to have the animal; he doubted it would live, considering its condition, but he would like to give it a try. He said that at all costs the seal must be kept dry and warm or it would surely die of pneumonia. He would send a truck as early in the morning as he could get one rolling.

There was simply no place for an adult seal at the laboratory; the only place available was a cold, unheated garage. That left me no alternative. I tried to soothe the animal, but she was nearly crazed with pain and fright. So I tried to lift her under the front flippers and was very nearly bitten in the process. Finally I did manage to wrestle a hold on her sinewy, writhing body, and, with a massive effort, lifted the seal into the back of my station wagon. I drove toward home, but over a hundred pounds of thrashing seal, rolling first to one side and then to the other, caused the trip to be a bit rocky.

Arriving home, I at least had the help of two strong sons. She was lifted with gentle care, but still she made every effort to bite. Finally, she was deposited in the only room in our little house capable of withstanding a pail or two of clear, warm water thrown down with some force: the kitchen. It took all of three pailfuls to clean her. When the water was mopped up, the seal was forced into a corner and was tackled by a barrage of towels. Finally dried off and beginning to get warm, her doelike eyes (of such great innocence, now washed of mucus) began to lose their look of terror. Warm and dry, her short coat of a camel's-hair color, with irregular and sparse brown spots, was shining. She still coughed, for she was obviously a sick animal, but no longer offered to bite. She was given a bed of clean straw taken in from a bale kept as dog bedding, and lay there, as incongruous in that kitchen as a lawn mower in Cartier's window. We washed her wounds and treated them

with peroxide. The seal refused food; we had cut up some strips
of fish for her. Then we left her alone in the dark, an act she
seemed to appreciate.

It had been a good opportunity to examine a seal closely.
You might say it is an experience you would prefer passing over.
But I have mentioned my preoccupation with mammalogy; for
me, it was an interesting chance. And by great good fortune I
have a wife whose intellectual curiosity is unlimited. Of course
she "objected" to a seal in her kitchen—what woman wouldn't
—but she allowed the seal in her kitchen, not so much for me,
nor to satisfy her curiosity, but for the seal. And she was soon
so enveloped in a mound of reference books that she had little
time to fret. We were all curious, and were soon immersed in a
sea of seal data.

Our Harbor seal was that which you might expect to find off
Sandy Hook, for it is the only seal found "regularly" south of
Nova Scotia. The seal, generally speaking, is a polar animal. It
is perhaps "midway" (for our purposes, anyway, although such
speculations are exceedingly farfetched) between the terrestrial
animals with which we are most familiar and the whales. All
three are equally "mammals"; that is, they have hair of some
kind, suckle their young, are warm-blooded, and breathe air.
In such ways are they equal to man. I am willing to agree, without reluctance, that man "leads the pack" of terrestrial animals,
in that his thinking capacities are considerably advanced over
those of his fellows. Man can "fly"; and now, scuba-rigged, he
can swim after the manner of fishes. But although he is remarkably adept, man's presence in elements not strictly in his own
morphological bailiwick is marked by the same awkwardness
seen in our seal. The whales, especially in their smaller forms
known as dolphins and porpoises, are the true masters of their
element. But seals, also, are extraordinarily adept, being able to
descend to great depths and to cover, in comfort and familiarity,
enormous distances of open ocean. Their food being fishes, they
are of course at home anywhere in a marine element. They are
thought to be the survivors of a second mammalian invasion of

the sea; the first, lost in the antiquities of time, having been the whales. The first seals known were from the Miocene; but that does not necessarily "date" their invasion, it only indicates that knowledge of earlier seals has not been uncovered. Unlike the whales, seals must come out of the water onto dry land to breed.

Seals are of the Order *Pinnipedia*, which includes the solitary walrus and two types of seals: the Eared seals, such as the California sea lion, and the Hair seals. The walrus is a great 2,000-pound "seal," having two large tusks, practically no hair on his thick hide, and no external ears whatever. The essential difference between the seals is that one possesses the obvious external ears, the other does not. Both have hair.

The only seal with which everyone is generally familiar is the "California sea lion," so supple and active that he seems to be made of rubber. He balances on his nose, claps his "hands" (flippers), is relatively intelligent and altogether charming. The Hair seals are stupid and backward by comparison. But they have one crowning glory, their thick coats are of prime fur, having great durability and a glorious sheen. The fur of the Eared seals is far less attractive.

"Our" seal was a Hair seal. Her hind limbs extended beyond her tail, her neck was short and thick. Being a carnivorous animal, she had prominent and sharp teeth. But ours was quite old, for her teeth were blunted, yellowed, and worn down. The Harbor seal—our own, as I have said—is the least attractive of all, being relatively drab. It is also small, in spite of its weight: only about 5 feet long. The other northern seals—all Arctic animals—are the Harp or Ribbon seal, widely striped with a large "saddle" of brownish-black; the Ringed seal, which is really spotted; the Bearded seal (which has a beard); the Hooded, which has a swollen proboscis; and the Gray, which is quite large, over 800 pounds. Most of them will occasionally be swept southward by currents, the Harp seal frequently being seen in the Gulf of St. Lawrence. Only our Harbor seal, however, penetrates as far south as the Carolinas. There are seals also in the southern hemisphere; Australia has an Eared seal, and recently we have heard much of the Weddell seal of Antarctica.

In our own cove, I had only once "thought" I saw a Harbor seal. But I have seen them close before in New Jersey at Asbury Park. As I watched gulls from the boardwalk, in an atmosphere of popcorn, salt-water taffy, and the tinkling music of a carousel, I watched a Harbor seal gambol just beyond the line of surf. And once or twice we have seen them, only dark specks, in the waters of the Atlantic beyond the barrier beach. In New England they are far more commonly seen, coming to the rocky headlands off Newport and Cape Ann to lie on the rocks in the sun.

Now our own seal lay on the kitchen floor, softly bedded down with straw. Perhaps she slept during the night, but her sleep, if she slept, was punctuated by repeated coughing. The next morning the aquarium truck arrived and she was loaded aboard. She went down the road and out of our lives as much a "fish out of water" as she had entered it. And "fish out of water," in this instance, is perhaps the best use of a cliché that I can think of. She might as well have come circling down on a flattened disk from Mars. Surely she did not belong here. And surely our experience in trying to help her was not all that fulfilling. But what is one to do? To be charitable "even to the least among us" is a good enough purpose; and the seal was ill, no doubting it. But perhaps, with creatures so far removed from our lives, it is better they simply be let alone. They surely cannot remember why they once left the sea. Nor can we ponder with much profit the reasons we stand erect on firm ground, eating apples, as I have just finished doing—here being the core to prove it.

Odd animals are not all so far removed from our local scene. Many are interwoven into our landscape with every bit as much design and harmony as the brightest, most enchanting bird that ever tamely came to your feeder. And yet they are "odd" to us. This is only because we don't know them—or don't care to know them—with the intimacy with which we know the birds.

In this way are bats "odd." Some people think they are revolting. Why? Because they are unknown. But none of this is our fault, really. They are nocturnal, they are retiring, and—much like the poor seal—they are from outside the confines of our familiar world.

On yet another anniversary of this January week, I was called to the telephone at eight o'clock in the evening. "Mr. Peterson," said the scarcely controlled voice of a generally altogether controlled young lady of twelve, "there is a bat flying around our kitchen!" It seemed that she was baby-sitting alone.

I reflected upon two things as I quickly got my coat and drove down the hill: 1) her even comparative calm was, for one of her sex, a remarkable thing in the face of such a "horrendous" danger; 2) she was no fool, so if she said it was a bat flying in January then, however unusual, it must be a bat. I arrived to find Ann quite composed—although the kitchen door had been carefully closed. We opened the door and there, indeed, was a bat. As healthy and filled-with-beans a bat as one could possibly desire. I felt just a little proud of my initial faith in this young girl. She said bat, and here was a bat. The animal continued to fly in very tight circles, for it was a small kitchen. Finally he tired and skidded into a landing on the stove. I put my hat over him, and the emergency was over.

Ann smiled the broadest, prettiest smile, and said, "Gee!" her eyes shining.

I said, "Let's look at him." And we both did.

He (for it was) was a male Silver-haired bat, *Lasionycteris noctivigans*. He is not a hibernating species as are some of our bats, but neither was he wholly migratory as others. He has been known, upon occasion, to "over-winter"; a state not at all the same as true hibernation. At any rate, here he was, usual or not. Out from under the hat and in my large hands, he certainly didn't look very terrifying. Ann remarked on how small he was. And he was. His wings were only a scant 12 inches, fully expanded, and his body was smaller than that of a mouse. His fur was brownish-black but was "frosted" by white hairs which gave it a silver sheen. It was as soft a fur as can be found, but thick and luxuriant.

The small animal's eyes were not only obvious enough to dispel immediately any nonsense about "blind as a bat," but were relatively both large and bright. Ann remarked that he even looked "intelligent." I suggested that this was a highly variable term and scarcely usable under any conditions not directly concerning relativity, but we agreed he did "look" as though he possessed mental agility.

His "wings" were not that at all, but only elongated fingers on arms and hands that were in every way properly cinq-pointed and normal but with a rubbery membrane between them. Ann was alert enough to see that his knees bent "backward" from our own. I explained that it worked better that way since he chose to hang upside down a good deal of the time.

Ann also asked how I knew he was a male, then gasped and said "Oh!" as she clasped both hands over her mouth. Confidently equal, I thought, to the needs of this particular venture into sex education and enlightenment, I said, "The male is always colored in this fashion, while the female is much more of a sepia brown." Ann looked disappointed. I went on. "It is also the case in all bats that their reproductive processes and organs are nearly the same in use and proportion as those of humans."

"Oh, yes," she said. And I knew she was stumped. She could hardly carry it further without putting a somewhat accurate stamp upon her progressive knowledge in this direction. But she was not entirely stumped, for she had (and has) a streak of genuine courage: she blurted, figuring to throw caution to the winds in a supreme stab at being grown up. "Do they have babies the same way?"

I saw the tremendous strain behind the effort, for her voice cracked at "babies" into a high soprano. "Yes," I said.

That was an exchange worthy enough for victory to be acknowledged by both sides, so, in mutual admiration, we returned to the bat. We discussed his food (predominantly insects, but I said I doubted her premise that he was hunting for spiders). I suggested that it was not unlikely he had chosen, sometime in the autumn, to hide in some crevice of the house. Perhaps—I said —the heat awakened him and he began to fly about.

What was I to do with him? I said, to the young lady's complete bewilderment, that I just happened to know someone who wanted him very badly. (This was true, for, by odd circumstance, not many days earlier I was in Cambridge talking with a friend working on a sonics program at M.I.T.; he said he was running low on the live bats necessary to his project.) I told Ann of the relationship between a bat's echo-location and the principles employed in man's use of sonar through electronic pulses. She seemed delighted—as she is a kind child—that the bat was headed for no tragedy but was to be used for Science, that opiate to the modern mind which, not unlike the bat, is usually either revered or despised through ignorance. I went off with the bat, and Ann to the telephone, to impart, no doubt, the excitement in lurid detail to her "nearest and dearest" friend.

My own telephone was put into action as soon as I returned home. My friend in Cambridge was indeed delighted with Ann's bat—so much so that he would trust no conveyance other than himself. He left early the next morning for New Jersey by car, and the bat was borne northward in the gentlest of hands by two o'clock of the following day.

A short sequel to my episode with the Silver-haired bat is perhaps in order.

The bat was taken to Cambridge to face banks of instantaneous cameras, oscillographs, sonic computers, and audio-recording devices. He was the first of his kind to be tested—most having been of the cave-hunting varieties. He performed with agile grace and lived to become a sort of elder statesman among bats, having lavish praise heaped upon him from visiting scientific dignitaries. I have innumerable pictures of him. Really, I believe he was something of a "ham"; he seems to have enjoyed the entire affair.

This jutting-out, extreme northeastern point of New Jersey has been a comfortable niche for many centuries. It is quite reasonably temperate, not only in climate, but in elemental hazard in general. There is no tornado belt through its heart; earth-quakes are practically nonexistent, as is volcanic activity; and it knows neither mud slides, inundation by flood, nor (in historical times) complete devastation by fire. In prehistoric times, it is true, the sea had most of New Jersey awash. Sometimes, still, it is politically awash. But in the recorded history of this corner of land, a general prevalence of moderation and accord are to be found. Even the generations of local Indians who predated the white colonial invaders were among the least warlike of the American tribes.

I have mentioned the kitchen middens on our shores. There is yet another, very close to our house, toward the water; and the hills are crisscrossed with Indian trails worn so deeply that they seem to be elemental grooves permanently pressed into the earth. The Indians native to these hills, whose uncounted steps pressed our trails into being, were of the large Algonquin Nation, and of a tribe within that large group called the Lenni Lenape. Even this tribe was a large one and was divided into three clans: the Unami, meaning the turtle; the Unalachtgo, meaning the turkey; and the Minisi, whose totem was the wolf. The clans embossed their documents with these signs. The Minisi held sway over that region lying between the lower Hudson River in New York and the Susquehanna River in Pennsylvania. The Unalachtgo extended southward into Delaware; and the Unami covered most of what is now central to northern New Jersey, including of course our own lands of the Navesink. In fact, the very name of our local "river" and village is derived from the local sub-clan or community of the Unami, the Navesinks. Other local communities were the Toponemese and Machapoucks, quite nearby. But the great chief of the entire Lenni Lenape was traditionally the chief of the Unami, and the location of his seat of authority was in this Sandy Hook area. Possibly he was of the Navesinks and lived in our own little cove; certainly, even then, it must have been a highly desirable site, as the kitchen middens would seem to indicate. But such is only conjecture. The white settlers have lumped the entire tri-state group together as the Delawares. The fact remains that for untold generations this land was fully inhabited as it is today.

The highways which today interlace this state are nothing new, only wider. Many were Indian trails as well marked and as well known as anything modern. The Burlington Path, which ran from Wilmington, Delaware, through Burlington and Freehold, New Jersey, was one; and another was the Minisink Path, which began at the Minisi council headquarters on Minisink Island in the Delaware River and entered our own Monmouth County at Henninger's Mill in Marlboro Township. There are many others that were all arranged in a tributorial fashion to feed into the principal council area which was here, in the region of Sandy Hook. Such paths were in actuality "public highways" for the Indians, being open and free to anyone of even vague tribal or national linkage.

The first settlers have given indication in various writings that our local Navesinks were attired ". . . in Deere skins loose, well dressed (tanned leather) . . . some in mantle of Feathers, and some in Skinnes of divers sorts of good Furres. . . . They had red Copper Tobacco pipes, and other things of copper they did ware about their neckes." They had seafood, presumably in unfathomable abundance, and venison, turkey, and ". . . dried currants, greene Tobacco, hempt, and great stores of Maize (Indian corn) whereof they make good Bread." All things considered—not to disregard the generally acceptable nature of the weather (unlike the hard winters of the north or tropical summers of the south)—the pre-colonial life of the rightful inhabitants of these lands must have been enviable.

This "land of milk and honey" first had sand thrown into it, and began to turn sour, upon the first known "claim" by John Cabot in May, 1497. He stepped ashore thinking it was "Asia"— and it would have served him right if it had been, and those cultured inhabitants had forthrightly skewered him for all his running about "claiming" the entire land for Henry VII of England. Which is exactly what he did. But it wasn't Asia, and off he went, full of claims. Verrazano did much the same thing, followed in time by Estevan Gomez and Henry Hudson; and, finally, a small colony of Dutchmen dispersed themselves in a radius, made more "claims," and started to chop down trees and to build the embryonic beginnings of what have become supermarkets. The Indians, being of a peaceful sort, tried at first to live in harmony with the settlers, but the same frightful business of exploitation and greed that has not since subsided began to cause them considerable grief. There is ample proof of "legal" sale of lands by the Indians for all manner of goods. It is all just as legal as you please, as many a surviving document attests. The entire Highland peninsula was bought for some dry goods, some blankets, some coats, one gun, one cloth cap, one shirt, twelve pounds of tobacco, and one cask of wine. Not bad. The Indians were soon deeply suspicious (little wonder!) of the Dutch and preferred selling to the English, since selling seemed the thing to do now that things had turned rotten anyway. "Claims" and counterclaims were rampant in every direction, but the Dutch held it all as "colony." The Indians must have felt much as we do today who suddenly turn a familiar bend in the road and see a yellow bulldozer making ready to destroy yet another lovely orchard. Surely there was talk, then, of rising up and throwing out the settlers, as today we may think fondly of igniting the demon bulldozers with gasoline and seeing them melt into a pool of nuts and bolts—but then, as now, such puerile defensive action could lead only to trouble. And so Lenni Lenape turned the other cheek, were ever so gently eased out of their birthright, and began an ever-shortening descent into oblivion. This is not to castigate the Dutch, who not only prospered but who have survived. This is simply what happens. A heritage is exchanged for Progress. It is happening today in exact measure as it happened in the past. Someone always gains, and of these gains we hear much. Often there is loss. History, however, is written by the one who profits and survives, and loss is often difficult to compute in its magnitude. Often we never learn of it, and the twilight of history's truth passes into an eternal midnight.

Certainly there are some few survivors of the Lenni Lenape Indians. It would follow that some might not have entirely faded from the earth. Most, however, are gone. Only their paths remain (and then only in the most altered of states), a certain number of their village sites, and no few numbers of their artifacts. Museums contain certain good examples of the tools, household goods, even the clothing and amusements of the Navesink Indians. But museum specimens, although of value and interest, somehow all have a sort of Tutankhamen mummified essence about them. "Everyone's dead," I once heard a child exclaim in a museum. In line with this thinking, one of the most interesting experiences I have had locally is one in which the Navesink Indians were "brought to life."

I was standing at the marble counter of a local drugstore, quietly enjoying a properly old-fashioned "counter" Coca-Cola, made in precisely the proper way with the proper ingredients, all in a bona fide Coca-Cola glass lovingly settled into a genuine, worn, nickel handle—and all for the staggering sum of five cents. I mused deeply on the value of that one five-cent piece I had put down—value to me. It was money well spent. I noticed that it was a Buffalo nickel, and casually mentioned to Mr. Antonides, the druggist, that I saw fewer of those these days.

He said, "Well, I guess you're right, they're getting scarce— but yesterday I got in an Indian-head penny." And he put a finger into a cigar box and retrieved it, putting it down on the cool marble of the counter.

We both stood there and mutely looked at it. "Sure enough," he said.

"Yup," I said, with no obvious intent to imitate Gary Cooper —which, speaking of Indians, seems appropriate. I certainly don't normally say "yup." (Neither did Gary Cooper.) We were both feeling homely and rather "local"; much as the local hardware fellow who has never, by admission, been further north than Hudson County, New Jersey, speaks with a distinct "down East" twang. The druggist asked if I were interested in Indians. I said yes (having noticed my reflection in the mirror when I'd said "yup" and thought what an ass I was). He went on—"Well, if you're interested in Indians, here comes just the guy to tell you about 'em." ("Guy" is to New Jersey what "pard'ner" is to the West, and "bloke" to the United Kingdom.) The "guy" came in, carrying two large cigar boxes.

He was introduced as "this old-timer," and I with my proper name and a sort of bow (this hinging on the precipitous amount of my drug bill which I had just paid). The old man was nearly eighty, he said, and had been collecting "Indian stuff" for fifty years. The cigar boxes held the choicest of his arrowheads and artifacts, which, from time to time, he carried from store to store for nothing but the edification of an appreciative audience. He was never known to have sold one. He just "showed 'em around." He let me poke into his treasure, but only under an alert eye and under the condition that each be identified and explained by himself. I was delighted to have him go on and on. He explained how next to such-and-such a street (leading past a junk pile and an auto-body works) there was an empty lot which he was excavating and sifting foot by foot with shovel and sieve. "Kitchen middens I calls 'em," he said, as though the term was his own. "Bet you don't know what them was," he added.

"Nope," I lied. And he went on to give me a most complete (and most accurate) history of the area. He still *walked* over every inch of Monmouth County, always looking downward for signs of Indians. And he did know his subject most thoroughly, with an enormous depth of understanding for his long-gone friends. I never saw him again.

Indians are gone from our hills now. It is late January and, again, the snow has come. There are tracks. But none of these are Indian tracks. One day our own tracks will no longer be seen. Perhaps all of this comfortably safe, gentle corner of the world will be turned under and destroyed. But also, perhaps, it will not be; there is hope on every side for salvation of things worthwhile. Perhaps it will be wholly saved, ever as it is tonight, with its woods and fields silently filling up with snow; a small corner nestled away in the bosom of hills, contented as a cat with its dainty paws tucked warmly under its breast. Old Vowavapon and Tocus, the Navesink Indians who for thirteen shillings sold their last remaining rights to these woods, might rest more easily in knowing that the pyramiding of profits did at last peacefully surrender to reason.

Mice are not the most pleasant of topics in human conversations. And if mice could talk it is not likely they would lavish undue verbosity on the comings and goings and propensities toward cheese manifested by humans. Mice live in our woods, as I have given indication by speaking of their tracks pitter-patted about in the snow. I have even mentioned White-footed mice. Yes, it is a *kind* of mouse, with—giving a splendid boost to the good sense of name-givers—white feet. It (this mouse) also has a white belly and a bi-colored tail, the under half of which is white all down its length. He eats whatever mice eat (which is not at all cheese, but native seeds, roots, and some small insects), and has white whiskers and a line of demarcation between the expansive white belly and his back which is a soft, fawn-colored brown (generally). He has large ears, two cutting incisors above and two below, and large coal-black eyes, and his name is *Peromyscus*. He is clean, noninfectious, industrious, and thoroughly American. And, as I say, he has white feet.

Another local mouse is the Meadow mouse, *Microtus*. He is followed by a tail of medium length which is dark on both sides. His hair is more coarse, rather longer, and of a color which when attached to human females is called by the local *salon de coiffure* a "mouse brown." He has small eyes, can't see well at all, and scurries about beneath tunnels in the grass. He is really a "vole," so easily confused with "mole"; they are of a size, but worlds apart physically. I shall not compare the two, for it would take a whole chapter, or a whole book, or a whole lifetime—depending on one's inclination. (Mine is to take perhaps a half-minute because I think that is the maximum I might get away with.) In a word, the Meadow mouse is a "farming" mouse, nibbling soft grasses and tender shoots. He nests in tussocks or in grass beds connected by tunnels. I really think he is quite a fascinating creature and I personally am enthralled by him. My leaving him (whose name is *Microtus pennsylvanicus*) is not of my choosing. But I doubt if I can continue with both him and you.

Pitymys is yet another friend of mine. But he is one only on great sufferance, and he is most assuredly no friend of yours. He is the Pine mouse. He has not, and never had, anything whatever to do with pines. He was named erroneously a long while ago. Worse yet, only recently he was placed in the genus *Microtus*. What future taxonomic juggling will do with him is a question. Meanwhile, he is himself, *Pitymys*, or at least that name will serve. In these woods he lives in dark tunnels under the leaf mold of the oaks. He is woefully short of tail, but his fur is long and soft and of a lustrous red-brown. Again, small eyes, as befits a tunnel lover (this not to be confused with the Tunnel of Love). It is generally he—not the poor moles—who devastates your garden bulbs from within the earth and causes certain flowers or shrubs to wither. When his tunnels underlie your favorite beds you may well be in for trouble. Otherwise he is harmless. The Pine mouse is everywhere round us, but, as I say, he is a miner. He, too, is a vole. Voles and moles? It sounds like Dr. Seuss.

Yet two other mice may sometimes be found in our woods. One is very rare: another vole called the False Lemming mouse. The absurdity of that name is particularly evident: here he is— an entity who is *not* something else! His Latin name, however, is euphonious and pleasant, *Synaptomys*. He behaves much in the fashion of the Meadow mouse, but his tail is only a shadow of something more substantial. The other is the Meadow jumping mouse, *Zapus*. He is very different, really rather kangaroo-like in form. He has quite large hind legs and smaller forelegs. He has a tail that is extremely long and, as he leaps great distances in his escapes from danger, he uses this tail as an aerial rudder with which to steer his landings. The white of his belly (for whatever status value it may have) is a more pure white than any other mouse's belly. Do you know, this is all very true indeed, but I shall agree that it is in every way ridiculous. And why do I say it? Because it is true. And you will agree that, in these times, that a truth—even such a truth as this—is better than none at all. This mouse has a light, straw-colored dorsal coat, and altogether is as attractive an animal as any in America, large or small. He is little known because he is a gentle "country" mouse, inhabiting country fields. Farmers know him well. He does no harm to anyone.

There is a "city" mouse, come to us only by chance. He is foreign to America. This is the House mouse, *Mus*, a native of Europe. Europe is clean, and deeply conscious of beauty. Europe's mouse is dirty, scaly-tailed, disease-carrying, and a thief. He is oblivious to beauty, a wastrel, a scoundrel, and a half-dozen more of good, round, salty names of disapproval. It is he whom you know, and by whom you judge all mice.

There are those who will cite the questionable aspects of a dissertation on mice. But mice are a part of the woods here— a part of us, by way of association, and by way of something not unlike a mutual respect (for they become quite tame). Therefore (as it has been succinctly put by someone who was not himself immune from reckless diversion), "Let us love one another and laugh . . . let us suffer absurdities for that is only to suffer one another."

February

The Owls' Moon

Somehow there is no demarcation line between January and February. Often there is a late "January thaw." Not this year; the thaw came last month, and we have been frozen like a haddock in ice ever since. In fact, there was a storm of some vigor at the end of January, and it continued into February for nearly three full days. Even now that the wind has subsided and "order" been restored, it still feels like January and looks like it. No relenting in the firm grip of the cold has been anywhere in evidence.

Owls seem to go with a February night. Even as I write there is the *sotto voce* grumble of a Great horned owl from somewhere in the depths of the oaks. This, for owls, is the time of mating, thus a crescendo in vocal arrangements. I cannot help thinking, during these nights, when the cold is so crackling in its intensity over the frozen blanket of icy crust beneath, that the ardor being displayed in the trees above must be of a remarkably high thermal degree. Ordinarily the Great horned owl's voice is not so clear and vibrant as in this passionate month of February. Everything else may be cold and dead, but for owls, eagles, foxes, and some of the others, this is a time for awakening, never mind the temperature.

We have other owls besides the great hooter. The little Screech owl, whose quavering voice is anything but screeching, is heard throughout the year. But not especially now is he heard. He is far more vocal in the spring and summer. Then we have the Long-eared owl, and occasionally they sit silently in the bosom of the thick green conifers, saying little. The tiny Saw-whet owl is a diminutive puff of feathers no larger than a robin, except that his head is big and round and he has piercing, yellow eyes. The Barn owl, that inscrutable looking mousetrap, all heart-shaped face and iron claws, is a year-round resident, often coming to the barn but never nesting there (at least during my own period of occupancy). The large Snowy owl of the far north comes to us only in cycles—generally only in winters of great dearth and scarcity of food in the tundra regions. He and the Short-eared owl are seldom found in the woods but only on the salt marshes or open flats near the estuary or the sea. The one remaining owl of which I have not spoken is the "common" Barred owl; perhaps, outside the Screech owl, the best known of any owls we have. For some reason quite unknown to me, we have never seen or heard one in these woods. The mystery is most perplexing for every one of the others has at one time or another visited us. But the Barred owl never.

The Great horned owl—who holds complete nocturnal dominion over these woods—nests in three places very close by. This is unusual, for they, as do most birds, have "territories" over which they hold complete authority; and the larger the bird, the larger the territory. But here, one nest is a scant quarter-mile from another. Of course, we are possessed of a great abundance of their natural prey, and perhaps the cornucopian overflow does away with territorial argument. They are not always vocally demonstrative; during certain periods of the mating season they are conspicuously silent, appearing like a wraith when they appear at all.

One equally stark and similarly bitter evening the great owls had begun their serenade just as they are doing now. But they chose, that year, to roost far closer to the house; only perhaps a bare 50 yards off. That is, one particular bird chose to be there. As late January ground painfully into February, the tempo and duration of his hooting had accelerated. Now, on this night, he was in fine form. I had gone out quietly, walking over the wet, matted leaves, and had seen him jolting up and down like a trip hammer, his throat feathers ruffling and contorting violently. His beak was open and his large, wide eyes cast back a silver speck from the moon's brilliance. He saw me well enough, and looked down at me as he hooted, my "hiding" behind a tree being of little avail. He paid little attention to me. I then carefully retraced my steps and went inside the house.

Later in the evening, I noticed an increase in volume from the owl. Then the sound appeared to come from different corners of the landscape, as though he were flying from point to point. Finally our entire family began to comment on the sudden increase in the noise outside. I left the house again and very stealthily slipped into the woods—with all the delicacy of a blind bull in a dahlia bed as far as the owl was concerned. It was obvious to me at once that our owl had friends. The woods were alive with hooting. There were two owls—I could clearly see them in the moon haze and starlight—in the roosting tree. There was a third to the north, close by, and another to the northwest. Two more were stationed to the east and south. A total of six Great horned owls, all exuberantly engaged in an owl "hootenanny." Each was at his "hooting post" and each was jerking up and down in great animation and (as my daughter said) "hollering his head off." Which was the female, I never did learn. Certainly one at least must have been, for when I tired of watching there in the cold, I began to be more bold. I came out and clearly showed myself in the open. No response; only continued hooting. I spoke aloud. Still no response. I raised my voice and spoke more loudly. I sang a song. Finally I hooted in imitation. Not one paid any attention whatever. As a final gesture I walked directly to the tree in which the two owls were sitting. I took up a stick, hit the tree with it, and shouted at them. They stopped hooting; the others continued. Then one flew to a tree not 30 feet away, followed in a moment by the other. They immediately resumed their wooing, or whatever the name for this strange procedure. As I turned to go back to the house I called to the family. The porch light glared, everyone came out, everyone marvelled; finally we all went in. The owls kept on. A half an hour later they all flew off together, took up stations high on an eastern hill, and started all over again.

I had never before witnessed such a display of boldness by these great birds, nor have I read of such a thing or spoken to anyone who has seen anything quite as blatant. I could easily have shot two and, for the amount of interest they displayed, had time to reload and shoot two more. They seemed to have no fear whatever. I have not since been permitted by any of them to approach at all close, much less to engage in anything so shockingly familiar as actually speaking aloud. Perhaps they objected to my singing.

Nighttime and owls reminds me of the nocturnal feeding tray. It sounds ridiculous, but we have a "night shift" that takes over the tray as the birds leave to seek out their night's roosting perch. Even before the birds are all safely "tucked in" the night shift is active. It begins with the White-footed mice. They can often be seen while there is yet light in early spring, but now, in February, it is well dark before they come. Two, perhaps three, run up the drain pipe onto the tray. They sit in that enchanting pose they have and crack sunflower seeds with their teeth, throwing away the shells, eating the kernel, then, in an instant, reaching for another. Sometimes, but not often, an opossum will come. But a night visitor who seldom misses his evening snack is the lardiest, waddlingest, most brash of raccoons. He is so fat he sags over the side of the tray in folds as nightly he stuffs himself on lard and suet. His black mask is in keeping with his thievery, for he is eating the woodpecker's suet. If you should knock on the window he will grudgingly move. But first he presses his greasy chin against the windowpane, leaving a spot. The outside of the pane is covered with his chin marks. Then he will lurch off down the drain pipe, "backing" and slowly disappearing like

a fireman in slow motion or a ship slowly subsiding into a welter of foam. Once he slipped and his enormous bottom made a "sitzmark" in the snow.

When mice have tired, the coon gone off gorged, and even the skunk has come and gone, having eaten the suet crumbs spilled by the coon, the last night visitor arrives. You can often hear him if you listen carefully: a muffled *plop*. This announces our late diner, the Flying squirrel. His soft fur is like a cobweb in its quality of gossamer fragility. He daintily sits to wash his paws, and most delicately opens his seeds. He carefully avoids rumpling his fur or crassly sitting on his tail, and his large black eyes and silken whiskers give him a look of extreme innocence. Unlike the others, he is skittish, and the slightest movement near the window sends him off into the darkness like a puff of smoke.

Upon thankfully rare occasions a final visitor has been seen to come to the tray. Twice a Screech owl came smashing down in a heap, wildly clutching at the White-footed mice. To our knowledge he has caught none, but then "our knowledge" doesn't go very far. Perhaps he sits high on a projecting limb of the spruce nearby and regularly dines upon our friends. Were this the case, we should feel obliged to stop all nocturnal feeding. Very likely there is an occasional tragedy, but a sense of proportion must be maintained. There is always a setting akilter of the scales when any outside weight, however seemingly beneficent, is added or subtracted from the natural state of balance. The ecological point of balance is just that: an arithmetic zero. Any tampering with it, however slight, many initiate a chain reaction incomprehensible to its often entirely innocent instigator. And yet we are all human, not computers of ecological data. We "mean well," all of us. Certainly the feeding of birds and animals is—like the feeding of famine-struck humans—meant to be an act of kindness. I hope it is. But again, one can never be certain.

The "day shift" at the tray this year has been pleasantly productive. Much busyness and an industrious flying-about of seeds has brought down from their overhead passing more than one Pine Siskin and a small flock of Evening grosbeaks. How pleasing is the soft perfection of the latter! Not because he is "rare," which, to a degree, he is—but entirely for himself. He reminds me that I never tire of the simple beauty of our American robin. Of course he is not a "robin" at all, but a thrush, as I have said. His black, slate-gray, and burnt-sienna coloring, punctuated by white, is in every way satisfactory. His song can be monotonous —but so can Bach, repetition having nothing to do with integral beauty. The robin's sweet warbling and robust presence in the early spring is my childhood's first memory of coordinate beauty in nature. And the Evening grosbeak has the same harmonious blending of perfection in visual perception alone. This grosbeak is not loudly patterned and brilliantly painted, but resembles more a finely etched poem most subtly printed on elegant, soft-hued vellum. It might be said that his "perfection" of which I speak is not all that complete: he has, literally, a "gross" beak. This argument might go far with someone else, but you see, I happen to have one myself . . . and then, Madam, there is Cyrano, Pinocchio, the tapir, the Proboscis monkey, not to mention the pachyderms . . . and Julius Caesar, Barbra Streisand, Mrs. John Singleton Ashby Derby-Jones, a certain Albanian who runs a delicatessen in Hackensack, Charles de Gaulle, and . . . you see, noses in the matter of beauty are a thing only relative. Grosbeaks (all of them, the Rose-breasted, Pine, Purple, and others) are all beautiful. I will admit to some slight prejudice, however.

Along with the grosbeaks earlier this week came the Gray squirrels. We usually have one or two running about, fitting in nicely with everything else. But none of these newcomers were my friends. They were interlopers who, in rank and insubordinate disregard of trespass, came over the hill from the Highlands (and they all had scrunched-up noses). Too much of anything is not a good thing. However much both a vile cliché and a platitude, this is true; and thus I refuse to put it into quotes or to throw it out, or do any of a number of things with it which

would make my editor happy. It is true. And particularly is it true of Gray squirrels.

They came first in ones and twos. They ate. They quarrelled. They ate more.

Then they came in threes. And *they* ate. And they quarrelled. They quarrelled among themselves, then they quarrelled with the first comers. All of which time the birds had to sit aside in the nearby bushes to avoid being stepped upon.

Then more squirrels came. They came until there were thirteen squirrels around the tray, under the tray, and on the tray, all bunched into balls, fighting and cursing (I presume), and dangling their tails over the edge. Seeds went down as though poured from a chute into a sack. Two days of waiting for them to go away brought no cessation of crunching molars and no going away.

Soon the dog was tied under the tray. Thirteen squirrels ringed the dog. The dog barked. Thirteen squirrels retreated a very few inches. Finally one, bolder than the rest, recklessly ran past the dog. The dog sat down. Three more ran by the dog. The dog lay down. And the thirteen squirrels ran around the dog at will, quarrelling, fighting. . . .

Finally, the next day, like the passing of a plague, they all suddenly left.

There are more ducks in the river now than in January—some thousands, and they make quite a show. Large flocks rise and settle for an instant, then rise again in a whirlwind that throws the water beneath them into spate. The sound of their wings makes a dull roar until they straighten out in flight; then they whistle. The smaller flocks, passing close by the trees over-head, have that pounding-of-the-air-with-feathers sound—faint, then loud, then faint again—that is less like "sound" than like an inner pressure on the ear. Then some others add to this a distinct whistle as the air passes through their stiffer feathers. The sound of wings is a sound seldom missing from late February's scene of soggy snow and some delightfully warm days interspersed with days of chill, cold, or wet gloom. February's end seems always erratic and unstable, and "good weather for ducks" it is.

The greater number of waterfowl now are the "bay ducks." Great rafts of them, particularly of Greater Scaup, or "Blue-bill," and Canvasback, are more and more active. But "paddle ducks" are also seen in numbers, particularly the Widgeon. Whether in large or small flocks, or in just bunches of twos and threes, as with the Ruddy ducks, the fever of northern trek is upon them. We—in our own estuary and adjacent bays and ocean fringe—are a "staging area," literally a basin, into which nearly all coastal migrants come before launching off for the next "long stop," which may well be as far as Maine or Newfound-land. Many, of course, stop in along the way on Long Island, Narragansett Bay, and the coast of Rhode Island, Martha's Vine-yard, and Cape Ann, but many also go straight through.

There is one duck that will never reach the open barrens of the far north. He was shot, out of season. The duck may be dead, but if Justice is borne heavenward on any gentle winds of chance, there should be rejoicing in the Elysian water-meadows of duckdom. For the duck was revenged with an amplitude that would give joy to any lover of Justice. But it didn't bring joy to me.

We were standing on the rise below the barn, watching the ducks. "We" consisted of a renowned scientist from the American Museum of Natural History—a member of all the leading ornithological societies, himself a leader in wildlife conservation movements both in America and on nearly every continent, and a qualified sportsman of undeniable repute—and myself. We were old friends of such long standing that no particular barrage of comment was forthcoming. Just a quiet bit of duck-watching, all for simple pleasure. "There's a new one," I might say, speaking of a Widgeon just apart from the flock.

And my friend would answer, speaking of the European Widgeon, "You're right, there's the rusty head. But you can't see gray in this light. The stripes are missing though." Just a quiet look-around in an idle way.

Then, beneath us on the road, a car stopped. From it emerged a young man with a rifle. Before we could cry out he had aimed through a 'scope, fired, and had killed a Canvasback that was standing on the ice. With his rifle still in his hand he jumped round the car, down over the causeway, tried to cross the rotting ice to where the duck lay, and fell into the water. Though the water was only 2 feet deep, he gave up the duck in disgust and turned to go back to the car. In doing so he saw that he had been observed. He then ran for his car, slammed the door, and was off in a roar of exhaust and low-slung vehicular screeching undoubtedly spurred on by the knowledge that it was a dead-end road and that we were in between him and escape.

But he wasn't fast enough. While I watched the startled realization and instant take-off, my friend had quickly run to his car and had blocked the narrow road with it. The fugitive's old car screamed to a halt and the two young men in it started to whine even before they piled out to confront us. Obviously we were not amused. They meekly gave us their names and we took their license numbers, telling them this kind of thing could not go on. Of course, we were also sympathetic, youth being youth. But a wanton breaking of the law for no good reason wants following up or it goes unchecked and multiplies itself a thousandfold. This kind of thing had reached a point of complete recklessness on our local shores; wild shots had entered houses, and one boy had nearly blown the hand off his companion—I had to help hold things together in a welter of bloody tourniquets until the ambulance arrived. This kind of nonsense had to end somewhere and we, both of us, were then and now firm advocates of the belief that misprision is a grave indictment. We had no genuine "authority." We took it: in the name of George Washington, the Continental Congress, the Governor's personal Bible (all politicians have them to swear things upon), and Mom's Apple Pie. The warden was informed.

Our reasoning was justifiable enough: we wanted it made known that this cove was to be considered by all and sundry to be under the full protection of the law; that the ducks—and people—under that law would not be assaulted or infringed upon. We had cause in the end to wish we hadn't.

As the gargantuan machine of legal power began to grind, we were alarmed at the number of charges placed against the boy. I forget the exact charges and their sequence, but they had to do with "Shooting out of season; shooting across a public road; shooting from a car; shooting game birds with a rifle; shooting baited ducks; shooting within so many feet of an occupied dwelling; for the breaking of local, county, state, and federal laws in this, that, or the other manner . . ." et cetera; all in a voluminous folio couched in the dread, dull gray tone of hopelessness that surrounds legal language. The case was taken from the hands of the game warden into the jurisdiction of a local judge, then to the County Court in Freehold. The Federal government was in on it because of the banding; local agencies of the government as well; and even the United States Army, because the guilty party was a soldier on leave and due to depart for a European tour of duty, and now his shipment was in danger of being delayed because of a "pending suit by civil authorities." By a chain of linkage stemming from some military commander under the heel of whose boot lay this poor unfortunate poacher, a message came through Heaven knows how many subordinates to the County Judge, to the local government, to the warden, and eventually to me, asking if some sort of legal maneuver were possible to permit the boy's leaving with his unit. I tried my best, but once the behemoth of government sets to masticating it doth chew exceeding fine. No one could stop it. On it went, until finally, I am sure, it blew itself into oblivion under the dusty filing case of some obscure county clerk.

All of this because one obviously healthily inclined young man chose, in his last days of civil freedom, to take pleasure in the out-of-doors and to do only what man has done for centuries, viz., to shoot a duck. Misprision is one thing; cocksure, quick-on-the-trigger judgments are another. It is a narrow line we walk, always, between help and hindrance.

In nearly every English-speaking country (at very least) the act of legal notice denying access to lands is called "posting." Violations of this act are equally universal in being called "poaching." November is the beginning—and I know for a fact they start far earlier—of the muskrat trappers, who continue during most of the winter while fur remains prime, season or no season. They are poaching, for our land is clearly marked in opposition to their presence. Legality set aside, it is a game of cat-and-mouse.

The poacher of muskrats is hardly a felonious type. He is "an American" (he will say), firm in his rights. "America is a vast country of unlimited resources" (goes his reasoning). "From the earliest colonial times, Americans have wrenched their living from the land and clothed themselves with the furs of animals. A good, strong, sturdy stock" (are these Americans of whom he speaks), "toiling and struggling," etc. "Why, there was Father Marquette, Lewis and Clarke—and how about Daniel Boone!" This, and more, he summons in righteous defense, if given half a chance. Such evocation is well directed, earnest, and even forceful when, as it sometimes is, used in a court of law. What juror could barefacedly deny the staunch splendor of Daniel

Boone! But, theatrically armed or not, poaching it is and poachers they are.

I have great personal sympathy for these men, however. They are, you see, the successors of Daniel Boone. They may be tied to humdrum mechanization for their livelihood, but on Saturday their hearts are free. Their "dog and gun at their side," they penetrate into the wilderness to "trap as their forebears trapped." And they add an extra thousand or so dollars to their yearly income into the bargain. Not bad for "private enterprise"? Quite right. The only trouble is that they often penetrate not "into wilderness" but into someone's back yard. And there is where the trouble lies.

The muskrat, one would think, might hardly be worth all this contention among principles. Quite right again. The muskrat is only a rodent and one of limited reasoning powers (he has, you would see, an excessively small brain case). He does no great harm, but certainly no great good; he dines on water plants, roots, and occasional hydrophilic (a splendid word) animals such as mussels. His coat is—I can tell you—lovely. The soft underfur is close and downy, while the outer guard hairs cast a silken sheen of great beauty. Muskrat? Even his musk (glandular bodies located near the tail, under the skin,) is pleasant, and intermingled with his silken fur it lends an odor of feral delight to this blade-tailed, fat little animal. He is, in essence, a diminutive beaver. He builds houses of reeds and, with his webbed hind feet, he swims with strength and sureness in his watery habitat.

The muskrat has his niche. Unlike his cousin the beaver, he thrives in the very path of encroaching civilization. He generally prospers, and is commonly plentiful. To kill him for his bounteously splendid fur is reason enough. To knock him stoutly on the head and take his fur is not, perhaps, a gesture of maximum regard between fellow creatures—but then, he shall have had the remembrance of an ample progeny left behind and you will be well rewarded by possession of his good, soft, strong, and durable skin. But steel traps are vicious. They are plainly just that. And the "Great American Trapper" has lost the gilt from his image: now he traps in shallows where, instead of drowning, the animal dies in agony; he "forgets" where he set his traps; his indolence causes him to leave his trap line for days and even weeks. Often have I found rotten animals still clutched in the jaws of traps. And one day I saw a muskrat lacking both a right foreleg and a left hind leg, each having been broken and gnawed off by the animal in a frenzy to free himself from the crushing iron vice. And so I confront the trapper and prevent his trapping. It is a bother, but it somehow seems worth the effort.

Our muskrat, by the way, is as dark as any I have ever seen. In inland marshes they are quite brown, a warm sepia. Ours are nearly black, and seem far more robust and luxuriant, though a shade smaller. They are, each kind, all of one species; that is, there is no taxonomic distinction between the two. But our animal, which lives in salt-water marshes (and thus, perhaps, varies his diet somewhat), seems far different from the inland muskrat. Perhaps it is simply local pride to think him special. But he is "one of us." And we mean to protect him.

The beach strip in winter is devoid of color. The wet sand is gray, the damp rocks are gray, the sky, too, as often as not, is gray. The sea may be gray, also, and generally is in mid-winter—but it is an ever-changing pattern of shimmering light. Rays of the sun, piercing through the heavy overcast, pick out patches of petulant, choppy ocean and light them as if with theater spotlights. Often the winter sea will be moving with only a rolling motion and will possess over its entire surface the thin luminescence of a milky opal. At other times its raging breakers roar like a herd of demented sea beasts, curling in gray-green fury to a great crest, as maddened bullocks poised for a scant moment at a cliff edge, then to plunge over in a wild, screaming disarray, tumbling over and over to lie flattened in the spume. The ocean is at other times nearly flat and silent, eddying round the breakwaters to cause a mere splash of foam, as water casually tossed from a bucket. But these quiet periods are rare. At most times it crashes and bangs and restlessly pounds against our Jersey shore; either gray and shining in patches of moving light, green jade in the five o'clock twilight, or brilliantly dancing in a flying dress of emerald green, showing ruffles of flashing white. Whatever its mood, the sea is cold now. One's eyes soon water in watching it, but the crisp tang of salt in the air is refreshing and clean.

The houses which cling to the shore are a motley group—but now let me digress for a moment. I have used "motley" twice now, I believe. I do use it from time to time. So will have you. This time I stopped to follow it up. We are right (you will be pleased to know) in our use of it. It seems that in the fourteenth century, in England, craftsmen made a textile woolen called "motley." It was widely parti-colored or checkered and was often used to clothe the professional fools or court jesters—you know the sort of thing, with one leg dark and one leg light. Always, from its origin, it was an incongruous mixture of variegated colors. The name was derived from *Mustela*, the Latin word for weasel—a name most apt, for the weasel (or ermine) changes his coat from brown to white in winter. During this change-over, for a short number of weeks, the animal's coat is irregularly spotted in brown and white, making him a very "motley" sight. One would not think that namers of fabric would be so perceptive to such elemental occurrences as the changing of coats in weasels—and yet that, too, follows in this case, for someone had to fashion the robes of royalty, and someone had to sew on their collars of "royal ermine." Undoubtedly these garment-makers had the misfortune of occasionally being sent (from northern Europe and Scotland) ermines not quite finished with their protective pattern change. Thus when it came to naming a variegated pattern, one of them suddenly smote his brow (as brows were smote in those days) and ferreted this gem from his musteline mind. (I refrain from saying "in otter-fashion," thinking it too much, which it is.) And so, you see, it is difficult ever to totally leave the world of natural history—even in the garment trade. . . .

Back to business: the motley houses are not only motley in color, they are more than motley in structure. "Motley," indeed, is a pitifully lackluster word to describe these houses, each of

which was built and painted according to the whim of its own-
ers, at different times and in different decades of taste. They are
so "motley" one is inclined to blanch. These houses are painted
in shades one might think unimaginable—faded fuchsia, char-
treuse, screaming-meemie yellow, *azzura* of an Italian sky (which
stretches the imagination even when seen in an Italian sky, over
Maggiore or Como—on these houses it is beyond belief), and a
particularly bilious mot-mot green. So that you will not be inclined to smite your brow as did the tailor fellow, I will explain
that "mot-mot green" is a greenish yellow-green hue, named
after the Motmot, *Momotus momota*, a brilliantly feathered bird
of the subfamily *Momotinae* found in the tropical forests of
Brazil. (As though anyone cared).

These beach-front houses are relatively new, within forty or
fifty years or so. Before that time there were large houses of
gray-brown cedar shingle with curving gravel drives, lovely
green lawns, ornate pots filled with flowers, and a circle of clam
shells artfully set in concrete to enclose a flare of scarlet cannas,
in the center of which was stuck a white flagpole with the nation's canna-brilliant flag flapping perpetually in a steady sea
breeze. Some isolated specimens yet remain. But most have been
sacrificed in the annual suttee of winter fires which break out
at this time of year. Driven by the strong winds, they are consumed more rapidly, once started, than any pyre of sandalwood
and ghee. It is a shame, for they are being replaced by these other
houses all stuck together like the egg case of a conch, or (even
worse) by the stomach-balm pink of new beach clubs and
marinas.

"The old days," of which old people here on the beach strip
speak in tones of regret and loss, were those that have been soft-
ened by the opiate passage of time. Then—in the middle to late
eighties—people were fondly wiping away tears for "the old
days." Looking into the future, *these* days—here, now—will be
the "old days." There is no use crying over spilled champagne
unless you happen to sit in it.

Champagne was clearly the local beverage in the years following the War Between the States. Newport was still a quaint

fishing village when Long Branch was the Monte Carlo, Marien-
bad, and Brighton of the "Jersey Shore." President Grant had
his summer White House there and was often to be seen bathing
in the surf. Gaily decorated excursion steamers, flags flying and
bands playing, came in to the Steel Pier at Long Branch, to be
met by magnificent equipages and liveried servants. The Very
Rich were there to a man; their "cottages" were of dimensions
near to castles, and their gardens, households, and really quite
glorious selves were pinnacles of attainment and grandeur. There
were games of lawn tennis and croquet and lovely little lemonade
parties on the lawns, which—in total disregard for those who
complain about alliteration—were also lilting and lively.

But none of this has "changed." It has only moved. Now the
Rich are somewhere else, that's all. Despite the imposition of
taxes, which dampened the fun more than a little, still, all is not
lost with the Rich. May they ever prosper! It is not they who
tear up the land and lay waste to it for profit, nor build in an
anyhow fashion, selling cheap, quick-peeling paint as they go.
Not the Rich, buckoes! But those who are trying to get that
way. Avoid them.

The Rich do have a fault. That is their fickleness. They are
willy-nilly in their attachments, building a castle here, a spa
there, and scattering their dear mounds of money with light
little kicks of the foot or dribbling it out as do small girls in
white sprinkling rose petals in processions. That is, the Good
Rich. The *Other* Rich stuff it into a great sack and sit on it,
like an egg, or let it flow in drab waste only into Foundations
and inviolate Trusts, there to forever sink into the ground like
an oil seep. And instead they could be having great, splendid,
noisy parties with gaily striped tents on the grass, Japanese lan-
terns, and continuously interchanging orchestras, whole roasted
pigs near a swirling fountain of champagne, petit fours, foie gras,
and multi-colored bonbons. It was the Good Rich who steered
themselves grandly over the wide avenues, went up the curving
drives, and reigned in good-natured splendor in their airy, light-
filled cottages at Long Branch.

Then they left.

It was a pity. Long Branch went into a decline from which it has never recovered. Sea Bright, a former gem set on the edge of a field of dancing water, is unbelievably forlorn in its dotage. Will there be a rebirth? No. Never. Not as it was.

And the restless ocean on this, now warm, February day comes on and on in its patient caress of this shore; gulls screech their creaking calls as they drop clams from a height to the stone jetties below. The sand is cast up in wide-wale ripples as smoothly placed as though formed by a giant harrow. The wavering line of tidal reach has left a clinking line of polished mussel shells, worn glass, and pebbles. There is no President Grant nor glowing sunburned throngs. Only me. And the boarded-up blind on the beach club window behind me, which has become loosened over the winter and flaps now in the wind. I tie it back with a piece of beach-tossed twine before I turn to leave.

Gull. Even the name has a euphoric languidness; as has "meadow," another buoyant noun. "Gull" seems in itself to float on a cushion of air. "Gull-winged" is aerodynamic perfection. And gulls are a poem in balance and effortless grace.

All such musing is dispelled in an instant if your windshield should suddenly be smashed and the inside of a clam plastered in every direction on your car. I once halted behind a car which obviously had been stopped for an emergency. A woman stood outside the opened door, shaking in fear and anger and bathed in tears. There was the cracked windshield, and there was the cracked clam. And there was the bomber: a Herring gull sitting in eager anticipation, waiting for us all to go away.

I have mentioned gulls dropping heavy clams on the jetties; it is all very pretty and—except to the clam—harmless. But gulls of all species have discovered that a highway crossing a bridge is a clean-cut case of the mountain having come to Mohammed. What better clam-cracker? And cars even go more slowly on bridges so the tires don't muck up one's clam.

The principal bridge I have in mind is that not unattractive long bascule arch crossing the Navesink at Rumson. It has very nicely conceived lamps, curving gracefully in alternate harmony of design. At times, dependent on the tides, each lamp top is occupied by one gull. And thus stationed, all facing into the wind, they are pleasant ornaments of eye-pleasing appeal. "See the sea gulls," is the cry. But at other times, equally dictated by the tide level, these lovely statues are wheeling and screaming and diving; then with mouths stretched wide over a great quahog clam, they mount to a height above the road, and let go . . . down it comes: crack!

"One gull, one clam" is a sporting proposition, even with a new car. But forty or fifty gulls and forty or fifty missiles—all *dropped with unerring* accuracy on the road—are a gantlet not within reasonable odds. I have never been hit (by a clam) but I have had to weave and dodge so in a manner of drunkenness that it is a wonder the law didn't enter into the business of ornithology. I have said that I have never been hit by a clam— "as yet" should surely follow; also, the term "whitewash," in local parlance, has nothing whatever to do with either fences or Tom Sawyer. And so, to us coast dwellers, gulls are something more than just aerodynamically well proportioned.

As the aerial bombardment of the bridge goes on with the surge and retreat of the tide, beneath the bridge the same kind of clams, and others, are being delved for by submarine methods. The power plant is a raw-boned, red-faced, sandpaper-skinned man with horny hands and arms like knotted clubs, and the tool is a clam rake with an enormously long handle. He works from a plain gray boat, fitted only with an outboard motor. Since law requires that certain methods be employed, thus it is done: primitive but with good result. The motor cannot be used to drag; it is but transportation to the clam beds. The rake's claws unseat the clams from their beds and they are scooped up by a wire net behind the claws. Simple and efficient.

These clam diggers, many of them, are a good example of New Jersey breed: unimaginably hardy, good-humored, and simply contrived. Often they are to be seen standing just off the channel on a sand bar, in a temperature of under 20°. Having dragged their boats over the ice, and with yet unbroken ice all round them, they break through and wade over the bar gathering their clams. Their arms are lobster-red between their gloves and coats. They sweat and steam, pulling and hauling the entire time the tide is with them.

Hundreds of bushels of both hard and soft-shelled clams are gathered each year; still there are clams in plenty. Only the threat of pollution would seem to mar this plentiful harvest; each year, as surely as the clams are brought out of the sand bars of the Navesink, the pollution count grows. The clamming has been on and off the restricted list. Now—currently—they are safe. Tomorrow's harvest is always in doubt.

February's end can be bitter and cruel. This year it is soft and calm, "like April," as has been voiced by nearly everyone around me today. This day awakened pleasant longings for springtime, as the sailor long at sea can smell the land. Now February's next-to-last night is still warm and pleasant. Outside, leaning against a tree in the darkened orchard, I see that the stars are bright and fleecy clouds drift slowly by as though each might wish to stop but had to press firmly on. These clouds remind me of a sailing boat just missing its mooring in the dark; how firmly does it reach out into the darkened, silent water beyond.

Having left the stars—only a few feet (surely) above the clouds—I come into the barn and with the window open for the first time this year have been peering down the barrel of my microscope, contemplating microcosm with no less wonder than moments ago I "waited on the car of ancient night" in letting my mind sink outward into macrocosm. The green felt of my large table absorbs the lamp's extraneous light and I see, in the darkened loft, only the small white circle of a world beneath me. Without, there is blackness and the night. I think of Hugo's quiet voice: "A bit of mold is a pleiad of flowers; a nebula is an anthill of stars. . . ."

March

Our Own Dolphins

Possibly the most painful use of clichés is in reference to weather. I will spare you even examples. But it is true, April does have showers, May has its flowers, and September has a harvest moon. And March does, indeed, and in fact, have winds.

It is not only the force of March winds that awakens one's consciousness of them, it is their temperature that is something less than enchanting. The wind which now blows is gusty, sharp, and penetrating. I had come up from the barn with my hat in my hand, for it would not under any circumstances, unless held there firmly, stay on my head. My trousers flapped, my nose was red from the cold, and my poor old dog had her tail tightly between her legs and her head low. Now, inside, the windows shake and rattle, and the wind sings in pulsing, broken chords, as though Aeolus had a sore throat but would grudgingly give it a try anyway, complaining the while. It is chill, lifeless, and damp. There is not the vaguest sign of a crocus.

There is no snow, now, at the end of the first week. But as March roared in with jaws agape ("Why doesn't he *say* 'Like a lion?' He couldn't be doing worse, anyhow"), LIKE

A LION . . . (thank you) . . . it is too much to hope that more will not come. Last year at this time there was very little snow—only a few inches—but what there was made it difficult footing, for it had melted some, then frozen, so that the world was one sheet of slippery glass. There was scarcely any walking on it at all, so completely porcelain-like had it become. But it became necessary to walk upon it so we tried, with major losses of equilibrium, recoveries, and again, near disaster. The dog dashed out in the fashion that greyhounds do, went splay-legged in all directions, and ended up against a tree, having to be dragged back on her side before she did damage to herself. It was a wild business for the children, who were speechless with excitement and were sliding over everything imaginable on seemingly invulnerable seats-of-the-pants, but under constant maternal reminder that seats-of-the-pants *were* vulnerable and not without a certain pecuniary value which they had best consider. They paid no attention whatever.

In the midst of this ice circus, it became necessary for us to use the car. We crept down the road and turned right, toward town, and of course got stuck on Old Maid's Hill (called Old Maid's Hill since two maiden ladies of retiring nature once lived in a house nearby; as good a reason as any). Anyway, we were not stopped, halted, or in any way otherwise detained—we were stuck, plainly and simply; no nonsense about it. After I had finished questioning the wisdom of the gods in having prepared all of this (swearing), I went off to the barn to get a shovel. There was sand, well enough, in a yellow barrel tipped sideways; and the staunch, forward-looking highway custodians had put a shovel there, carefully reduced in handle length so that no one would steal it. Someone had stolen it.

I cautiously set out across the orchard in no mood to be trifled with, and, abruptly—mood or no mood—was trifled with. If one is to be trifled with, let it be, I say, by something of no trifling dimensions—something hog-wide and great-footed; something fully round, glorious and scaly, and breathing smoke. Let it not be a mouse. My antagonist was—a *mouse*. He, also, had evidently had an altercation of some sort, for *his* mood was nothing to be proud of. I saw him before he saw me—which is not odd, for he was a Pine mouse, none of which can see very well at best.

He (this mouse) was swearing (I am not being anthropomorphic. Why is it that Man centers all about himself? I know more than one man who is rodentomorphic . . . but to go on). He, like myself, could not walk with surety on the ice. And he could not find *any* kind of a hole, mouse or otherwise, into which he could go down into a tunnel and light out for home. And so, he was in a temper. I could clearly hear him grumble as each depression was found to be covered with impenetrable ice. To that mouse, I was the last straw! When he became aware of my presence he grew furious, trying to hide with even greater energy. I had little fear of him—having gauged myself as just eighteen times his height. So with great pluck and determination, I set out to pursue him—all in the spirit of fun. And what did *he* do? He chose to attack me! Running some, he would wheel and turn, standing to his full height of 4 inches to squeak in a most irritated fashion. My persistence only made him the more angry. In turning to face me and to shriek, he became what must have been (to a mouse) livid: he sat and, literally, barked hysterically like a dog in frenzy, inching forward as he squeaked and ranted. Finally, he stopped. No doubt he was exhausted. I felt pity for him, so far down below me, still staunchly facing his nemesis. I broke with my heel the ice round a tree base and pushed him gently into the grass-lined cavity, hoping to protect him, at least, from a marauding bird. Down he went into the hole I had made. I could see him as I left, nose poked out in defiance.

Someone with a scientific turn may question the wisdom of letting the mouse go, arguing that because of his strange actions the tiny animal may have had rabies. Certainly he may have had rabies. And the cow pox and fleas beside. Nonsense. He was a mouse "fed up," as I was myself. He was giving vent to his spleen. He was behaving like a male. Man or mouse, when everything in a day turns into "one big fezzle," a good cuss is the only remedy applicable—and the only remedy that Woman will never understand.

Woodpeckers, mud, wells, and cesspools would seem to have very little in common. Not so. They have March in common. There was a wet snow the other day. Now it is gone. It is warmer. The crocuses are pointing green pins up through the soggy leaf mold and wet, brown grass. I saw an earthworm; a rather cold-looking and rubbery earthworm, but an earthworm just the same; banded near his heart, and whitish pink—liverish at best, but whole and sound after the winter. Woodpeckers are here all winter, at least the Downy and Hairy; and the black Great Pileated would be, but he is long gone from these woods. The flicker (ours is golden-shafted; that of the West, red-shafted on their ventral tail and wing feathers) migrates, but returns early. Now he has come back to us in force—the white flash of his dorsal rump patch (called "upper tail coverts") goes through the brown woods like a snowball as he springs from the ground in alarm. He is often on the ground to feed, but will nest in a hole drilled into a dead tree. Now he has come without a mate and is determined to find one. His persistent drumming beats a constant tattoo over the hills, and one has found the metal flashing on our chimney and works at it like a trip hammer to awaken an interest in the female breast. At first he was welcomed as a harbinger of spring, but a few days of percussion on that chimney flashing is enough to dampen the ardor of any bird enthusiast. Even worse, this muscle-necked moron, as often as not, hitches down the side of our house and, with reptilian stupidity, proceeds to hammer holes into the cedar shingles.

Woodpeckers have little to do with mud, but mud has much to do with March. The "Thaw" (like the flickers) is both welcomed and despised. Seeing the frost out is a joy—but seeing the frost *half* out, like Casey at the Bat, brings no joy to Mudville. With the frost (still firm a few inches down) preventing run-off, the ordinarily malleable, dark earth turns into a sticky paste. The flagstones sink into the earth with a two-inch ring of mud

surrounding them. One's feet become chocolate clubs, and mud, wet, semi-dried, and dried—is tracked in, dribbled off, and smeared on nearly everything. The road turns into a quaking chocolate pie with knife-cuts of tire tracks deeply incised in its crust. Then, of a sudden, as though a plug were pulled at the bottom—it all dries up, left with its scars of footprints and tire marks, but otherwise becoming just plain dirt.

The same run-off drains into our cesspool. A cesspool is now called a "septic tank." A good name. Being familiar with "anti-septic" as a good thing, one must logically conclude that "septic" must be less of a good thing. It is. Particularly when it over-flows. The person who says that such an occurrence is "good for the lawn," is the same who will say "ashes are good for the rug." Someone else will say, with nasal authority, that a cesspool is not the same as a septic tank. The *Cloaca Maxima* in spate is neither. But all have a sinister, familiar way with them that is better off underground—and March is not the month for view-ing them at their best.

Wells, too, (on the up side from the cesspool) make for interesting commentary in March. It is a pity that such commentary cannot be shared in what is coyly called "mixed company," for surely as a device for the enrichment of language it could have few equals. For wells, in March, have been known to acquire mud, or silt, or garbage, or whatever it is that plagues them, in the undergarments of their manifolds, carburetors, pistons, or what-have-you—causing them first, to burn out a fuse; second, to drop the level of water in your storage tank; third, to lose their "prime"; and fourth, to stop. The "well man" is called. He is "on another job." When he does come, he must "have a look at it"—"it" being at the other end of 178 feet of 2-inch pipe, which just happens to be straight down. The derrick is brought—and gets stuck in the mud. Two trucks come—and *they* become mired. Finally it gets done, a week later; during which time we have brought up water in buckets from Jack's house and filled the bathtub, the tank atop the john, three pails, an old fish tank, and every pot in the house.

Such is March, the Ides of which are past.

Foxes are as much a part of our landscape as the trees. There are times during the year when we wish they were not. Unlike many wild things, Reynard long ago found that, in the changing patterns of circumstances, he must either perish or adapt. He has adapted. He has probably even grown to like it, since change of any kind sharpens the blade of one's wits. Not that his needed any honing. Foxes have been clever (it is to be presumed) since foxes were fashioned. Aesop tells of their wiles, and untold generations before Aesop was a cub (which is what young foxes are called). Foxes are bright as a new penny in the wild, where they have already an array of fair-sized wits lined up against them. Where they coinhabit, cheek by jowl, with humans, they become even more crafty, more suspicious, and even downright Machiavellian in their intense determination, not only to survive, but to prosper.

And prosper they do; each year we lose some hens, a duck or two—whenever the stern, cold eye of watchfulness relaxes. We *know* this. Therefore the fault lies not with the foxes, but with us. In return, perhaps, for our *not* persecuting the foxes (however great the temptation might be) the foxes don't persecute us. That is, they take fowls—but *only* during that period of March and April when the vixen is hard put with a litter of cubs. At all other times they carefully avoid our hens, even to the point—as has been often the case—of walking right through a cluster of them, looking as smugly self-righteous as you could imagine. At other times, both dog fox and vixen have walked slowly under the clothesline as clothes were being hung, and blown flapping, and the wheel of the line connected with a tree was squeaking loudly. At one of these occurrences, I remember the audacious scoundrel looking up over his shoulder to "smile" that foolish-looking, tongue-lolling leer they have after a good run. At another, one had the infernal cheekiness to lie down at the edge of the grass—directly under the flapping clothes—and to stretch! Our dog, meanwhile, (this was when she was younger) would be in a fit of apoplectic frustration and vocal remonstration from her chain-length back by the chicken house. The foxes gave her not so much as a glance (knowing full well the exact length of her chain and the poor dog's perimetric latitude of dominion). As all of this testy familiarity progresses, it is very evident that it is the foxes' game, not ours. One movement from us that is even slightly out of the ordinary, and they are gone in a flash. We make it a point never to feed them. Our relationship is one purely of continued proximity. Thus do we "get on" with foxes. Our foxes are both Red and Gray. That is, there are two kinds, each quite different from the other. The Red is *Vulpes fulva* (and is called simply the Red fox). His red is rather orange, lightly intermingled with Venetian yellow. The tail is topped with lighter hairs, the ears are backed with black, and the legs and feet are black, as though with pulled-up old-fashioned stockings. He is dainty and most vainly considerate of his precious, silken coat of long, fine hairs.

The Gray fox, *Urocyon cinereoargenteus*, is not quite as saucy and perspicacious as the Red, or it seems, at least, to be that way.

Not that he is "retiring"; hardly that, but there seems a differ-ence somehow in "verve." There is nothing definite I can cite in this, just long years of relationship. It is an acquired attitude on my part. This fox is not by any means drab, as "gray" might seem to indicate. His back is "salt and pepper," the hairs being banded with black and grayish white. The inner sides of the legs, the belly, neck, and a band across the chest are of burnt sienna (a rather pleasantly autumnal soft, reddish-brown). The sides of the nose and under the muzzle are black. The tail is grizzled, as is the back, but has a concealed "mane" of stiff black hairs. His fur in general is far more stiff and coarse, completely lacking the silken qualities of the Red.

The Red is mostly a northern animal, while the Gray is far more of a southern fox, only within recent times having ex-tended its range into parts of New England. Their diet varies greatly, but, being carnivorous, the food of each is based mostly on mice, rabbits, and other such animals and birds, but will often include fruit, snakes, turtles, and eggs. The Gray, in par-ticular, has a heavy propensity toward seafood, eating nearly anything of the sometimes heady *bouillabaisse* of offal thrown up by the tides.

The reason for my bringing up foxes now rather than wait-ing until April when their presence becomes a matter of more than passing interest, is that this season brings out the fox hunters. Now in this reference I do not mean the Hunt (which is gener-ally 95 per cent "chase," 4 per cent "miss," and perhaps, part of 1 per cent "fox.") In our woods the threat comes by the com-bination of dog and gun. The packs employed are far from the elegant harriers of the Hunt's kennels; they are, more often than not, mongrel curs of hound ancestry, the sight of which is revolting and whose yelping cries are an anathema to me. Upon occasion, however, some hunter will have a fair enough beagle or two; but in these, too, the yelp is high-pitched and often hysterical. But there is one poacher—whom I loathe— who has a few large black-and-tan coon hounds. These have a deep, full-throated bay, resonant and beautiful; as haunting a song in the moonlit stillness of a still-sharp March night as ever raised the flesh of one's spine.

The essence of this tale is that on one gray Saturday afternoon a few winters ago there was the usual midwinter baying up and down these small valleys, now close, now far away. Suddenly there was a rush of dogs on the hill above our house, and a loud report. I was running hillward in a matter of seconds.

The hunter saw me coming and began to run, but he was burdened under the weight of two dead foxes, one Red and one Gray. Finally, after a mile or so, I outran him—but in the chase we had both run well off our land and onto someone else's. The hunter was an old hand, well under my size, and also, being desperately winded, was inclined to be agreeable. My rather picturesque language and more than a little blood in my eye probably did more to convince him that I meant business.

I said, "Those are my foxes and I mean to have them, and you, too." I then pushed his gun aside and grabbed the foxes. This was no heroic action. I was simply in a dreadful temper. I

said harshly and in a voice of much authority (an authority I did not have, its being then, as I say, someone else's land), "Follow me." And he meekly got into line behind me and we wound down through the trees over the crusted snow.

I rested once or twice, the two foxes becoming heavier with each difficult step through the snow. Then I noticed the hunter was no longer behind me, but had turned and was running away. I sat down on a stump and laughed. What children we both were! I, in my ridiculous temper, shouting and ranting like a schoolboy! I didn't "own" the foxes; nor did I even own the land—though a friend of mine did. And that other poor fellow: —running away! all because he had no land of his own and nowhere to go. What a chronicle of the picayune, I thought.

But there were the dead foxes. I carried them home. What does one do with a dead fox? Ordinarily, nothing. Skinning them is all too much trouble. Fur is worth far less than you might think (the great prices you pay going not to the hunter or trapper, but to the people in between). Having two dead foxes, then, you simply throw them away. However, I could scarcely do that; they were not only "my" foxes, but were simply too beautiful to let rot, and the ground was too frozen to permit burying them. Put them in the trash to end up ignominiously in an incinerator? Hardly. I had never in my life done that. I began to wish I had never seen either the hunter or the foxes. So I prepared them in the form of museum study skins and they went into a collection with others of their kind.

There is no moral. Two of our foxes are dead, but there are others which remain. I am often inclined to feel foolish after such an incident; feeling like a toothless old dog who is too winded to bark and can only totter off in the direction of danger, doing no good whatever. After the shot is fired, the damage is done.

No great influx of any mammal is ever in evidence in our waters. When seals come, they come singly. Muskrats are hardly maritime. And few others, except for a short swim, (such as a mink in pursuit of a fish, or a deer in hasty escape) really spend much time in the water unless they fall in permanently. But, occasionally, we will see something that strikes the imagination.

That something is whales. It is the sight of these mammals even without a knowledge of them that is moving. When dolphins (also called "porpoises," though they *are* whales) come in to the Navesink, cars stop bumper-to-bumper to watch them, children are brought long distances to "see the porpoises." No trained actors, these, but wild animals—whales. Not often do they come, but they do come.

A few years ago three dolphins were seen near our cove. Then they appeared in various places at various times and finally settled down in and around our cove and the Rumson bridge. They stayed for many weeks. People thronged to the quaysides and along the curving causeway leading to the bridge. Children were propped on the railing, and cameras and binoculars and loud cries of "There they go!" were to be seen and heard on every hand. On Sundays a policeman had to come and sort the people from time to time.

Far from an expert in marine matters, I was nonetheless as fascinated as anyone, myself going to the causeway to gawk with all the rest. However, I had been in contact with another mammalogist whose field this was, and his interest was keen. I began, then, a serious study of these warm-blooded compatriots of fishes, mollusks, plankton, and whatever else is foreign to our homely, fireside kind of life.

"It is cold and wet down there," I remember saying as, alone and in gray weather, I knelt by the bridge and looked into the water. Geoffrey Tate, a friend of mine, well-informed in a variety of things, had told me of his having swum with dolphins in these same waters. He'd gone, he said, right down among them, and they had touched him with their noses and had frolicked with him in the waves. Their intelligence was reputed to be high, although to me—at that time—their wet backs were the most I could see, and no more than a splash could be heard.

I had first become interested in these animals when, having to travel great distances in open schooners between islands off the coast of New Guinea, I had lain by the gunwales for long hours watching the dolphins in the crystal waters. I had been fascinated by the seeming intelligence in their eyes as, only a few feet away, they swam in effortless motion in the green break of the bow wave, playing with the boat. Also, in Australia, my wife had become enchanted with a dolphin kept in a local marine aquarium; she used to sit and "talk" with it as it came to the edge of the pool, and to scratch its head and pat its nose.

Now—some years later—a great deal more has been learned about dolphins, and our amazed reactions of the time seem amateurish and hopelessly elementary to even the very young. A wide public interest in these animals has developed as a result of scientific disclosures having been sympathetically reported in the news media, and, even, by commercial facilities of public entertainment. Dolphins have been proved to have an intelligence far in excess of that which was suspected. They have been proved capable of learning many things, and much has been done, even, toward decoding their language—for it seems they do "speak" under water—and, in correlating the intricacies of their remarkable powers in submarine perception. With all of this, it becomes increasingly difficult to remember that in their natural state they are still "wild animals"—not carefully coached soloists.

The dolphins in our cove were wild animals. They seemed far more akin to great shiny-backed, wet fishes than to anything warm-blooded and friendly. I persistently followed their movements and ascertained that two were adults and the other a juvenile, although the young animal was nearly full size. It was obvious that the young was cared for by the other two—presumably parent—dolphins. They would often turn course to give gentle attention or nuzzle the young softly; never with any harsh motions.

They swam in slow undulations, plainly feeding on fishes, and before too long the local fishing people were in vehement condemnation of them, calling for "measures" and loudly trumpeting their "rights." Then shortly, from within their own ranks, came a direct reversal of their objections: the fishing, they found, had never been better—and the dolphins were then loudly praised for having the effect of "stirring up" the fish to greater hunger. The general public, too, became convinced that the dolphins' dorsal fins were not the horror billboard advertising the shark, but that they were harmless and worthy and all the rest. The local newspapers divested themselves for a moment of their dreadful glut of mediocrity and, rising gloriously on their own petards, proceeded to chant hallelujahs of gladness in support of dolphins. More cars came, full of people, and howling progeny, eating popcorn. They were "happy times"; everybody could see—and the dolphins were unaffected and safe from too much affection.

It all lasted for a surprisingly long time; most of the winter, in fact. Then, with the coming—in late March—of softer airs and warmer waters, boats came out of their winter's sleep. And with the boats came powerful outboard motors. And with the motors came boys; and with the boys were rifles. With these motors the dolphins were chased in sharp circles, and the police chased the boys who were chasing the dolphins, and angry letters were written to editors, and editors wrote editorials (as they are prone to do), and *more* people came to see the dolphins and to see the dolphins be chased. And then one of the dolphins —the young one—was found dead. Its tail was badly gashed, as though with a sharp blade, and it had two small holes from which blood ran down its back.

There was a reaction. More angry letters. A sign was erected, imploring the public to "Protect our Dolphins," explaining what they were and why they should be protected. The Coast Guard was called about the dead dolphin. They came in a cutter and tied a line to its tail and began towing the body seaward. The remaining dolphins (I was told in detail by the Coast Guard officer in charge) stayed close by during the operation of securing the dead animal. Then they swam with the boat, one on either side of the dead one, in evident purpose of lending support to their young. It was said that it was a pathetic sight, for they seemed in every way trying to help. They followed alongside for some miles into Sandy Hook Bay before slowing and dropping back. Then, still, they followed, swimming abreast, for some miles further. Finally, they were seen to turn and fall behind the boat.

Later, the two dolphins were again seen in our cove. They took up their fishing as before. People still came. More boats chased them. And then another was found dead, shot through the back. On some of the cars were signs reading "Protect the Rights of Americans to Bear Arms." It is not unlikely the same signs will be found in Dallas. Surely they are much in evidence here. Any twelve-year-old boy can, with complete impunity, wander about anywhere with a .22-caliber rifle—considered by many parents a "right" of the child, like erector sets and electric trains. And so things are shot from time to time. The second dolphin was towed off by the Coast Guard because, although killing goes well enough with the American's "rights" about which he speaks so much, putting up with the stink after death is not part of the bargain. I know a specific instance wherein an animal was slaughtered by a boy with a gun, and his parents were the ones loudest in complaint against the town's laxity in disposing of dead animals. The dolphin, at any rate, was taken to sea and cast adrift.

Less than a week later, as I drove over the bridge toward the children's school, there below me—only a few yards from where stood the "Protect our Dolphins" sign—floated the body of the last survivor. The American Museum of Natural History, being in constant touch with me in the matter, had requested that in the case of another being killed I might do an autopsy and keep the head for them. So, on this cool day in late March, I set to work.

I engaged a cooperative clam digger for the use of his boat in helping me secure a line to the tail. We dragged the dolphin to a small beach and I took photographs, some measurements, and notations of its injuries. This was the female; she had been shot twice, once in the back and once in the head. The low puncture in the back had punctured a lung and a bubbly froth issued forth. She was (as were the others) a Bottle-nosed dolphin, *Tursiops truncatus*, the same kind found so tame and so charming in oceanariums. She was about 11 feet long, dirty gray in color, and was scarred and not in the best condition (aside from being dead). She had forty-six small but very sharp teeth, and it was easily seen how she could catch fish with such a sharp vise. There was a transverse groove between her 3-inch beak and her rounded forehead. Her tail (or flukes) was "sideways" to that of fishes, as in all whales.

I turned her over only with great difficulty (even with the help of my clam-digger friend). I detached the head (which was an operation not dissimilar to cutting apart a whole watermelon—except for certain incisions to separate the vertebral column at the base of the skull), made a lengthwise ventral incision, and probed for the bullets, finding them to be .22-caliber-long rifle slugs. I found little out of the ordinary in a pathological survey, then poked about a bit more to find that she had last dined upon Croaker (evidently from round the pilings) and what looked like a large Killifish.

By the time I had finished and the water and sand were discolored with blood and gore, I started to leave. As I staggered off with the bloody head—which must have weighed fifty pounds—cars began to stop on the bridge above me and two elderly ladies came to the edge to berate me for "doing such a thing."

"Madame," I started to explain, "a museum has requested..."

"You ought to be ashamed!" they ended together as, caked with a mixture of salt water, blood, and sand, I reached my car and drove off. "We ought to turn you in," I heard in the distance, "... the idea, mutilating the poor thing like that!"

This time it was I who called the ever-patient Coast Guard. I said to the coastguardsman who answered, "There seems to be a dead dolphin by the bridge." And I have since wondered exactly what passed through their minds when they found it to be without a head.

My next problem was what to do with the head, which had begun to reach a state of aromatic richness—not of putrefaction, but simply a heady combination of fish-smell and blood. Which stank more, the head or me, was a question. I found it too large for my freezer, so was confronted by a real problem, as it was a Friday and the museum truck could not come until Monday. I chose to wash both of us (the head and myself) carefully, then wrapped the head in newspaper and in a double layer of brown paper. I then went to the manager of a supermarket in town and said, with a very great measure of truth, that I had a very large piece of meat which would not fit in my freezer. He asked what it was, and I replied that it was very heavy.

"We're not supposed to . . ." he began.

I said, "Just until Monday." He finally assented, no doubt with quick mental calculations lending support to the theory that if it were my mother-in-law, I should hardly want her back on Monday morning. Feeling rather like Robert Montgomery in *Night Must Fall*, I guiltily handed over my package, mentally composing excuses vaguely built round "all in the course of Science." The truck came Monday and departed with the head.

The smaller Harbor porpoise, *Phocoena phocoena*, also comes into our waters; but the more pelagic Atlantic White-sided dolphin, *Lagenorhyneus acutus*, does not. The much larger "Blackfish"—*Globicephalon melaena*, a whale over 20 feet long —has been known to be cast ashore on the barrier strip. So much for "little" whales.

Just a word more on whales—the Fin-backed whale has also been washed up on the Sea Bright beach, as has the Sperm whale. Only a few years ago a small Sperm whale (the Moby Dick sort, but black) was washed ashore at about the point where the birds are killed by wires. There is a very narrow beach there at low tide. The animal was alive when it came aground—with, again, seemingly a propeller gash on its flank—

but died shortly afterward. I had seen it for a brief moment and then had to leave for a day or so, during which time a strong current had prevented the Coast Guard from their usual unenviable task. The whale lay there still when I returned.

The two days or so of sun plus the natural forces of decomposition had changed the whale from an object of interest into a mountain of putrefaction. I had seldom ever smelled anything quite as powerful. While it had been still reasonably fresh (it can be presumed), someone had sawn off its thin lower jaw containing the conical, ivory teeth. And someone else had carved with a knife some initials and an obscene word into the flesh, exposing the white blubber beneath the skin. As I climbed down the sea wall to approach the spot where the whale lay, it was like a blow in the face; a stink so heavy that the surrounding air itself seemed to have gained in weight, as in a supersaturate solution of liquid. It was a thing even beyond nausea, seeming to affect even the fibrous cavities within one's nose so that, days later, the smell and taste of that dead whale remained. The heat from the decomposing blubber was felt even many feet away, and innumerable flies were hovering and buzzing in an orgy of frenzied delight. I quickly sought the windward side, but even that was contaminated to the extent of being impossible. I turned, as had everyone else long since, and fled. What the Coast Guard did to free the whale's rotting carcass or how they towed it out to sea, I do not know.

Bats have been mentioned. We have other bats, but no great profusion of them. One is the Silver-haired, of which we spoke. Another is the Red bat; a bright orange in the male, while the female is a duller brown-red and has some white sprinkles too, as does the Silver-hair. Yet others are the Pipistrelle, a grizzled yellowish-brown, the Little Brown bat, and the Big Brown bat —both a sepia brown, different in size and character. All are insect-feeders. The Silver-haired and Red bats are "generally" tree bats; the others seek caves or (here) houses or garrets. The presence of each on warm summer evenings is pleasant. They do no harm, and cartwheel through the trees in vigorous pursuit of their pestilential prey. Therefore, they should be looked upon as "good." They are, by us.

But the time for bats is not yet. Later, in late April and May, we shall see them in numbers. One bat, however, was with us today. I had come out of the barn to run with the dog—and to "run myself," having been sitting, cramped, at a table for some long hours. In the late afternoon's sunlight I casually noticed the warm fading sunlight strike red on a flying "bird." A second glance showed it to be no bird, but a bat. It was a migrating Hoary bat, the largest (having a 16-inch wingspread) of any North American bats. He is narrow of wing and swift of flight. His fur is mahogany-red and "frosted"; it is thick and soft and lovely; and under the chin it is cream-colored. Certainly he is our most beautiful bat. He was not flying at his usual speed, but more slowly, and in great wide circles over the wide expanse of lawn and the orchard. He flew, then, in broad daylight (though light was fading) and was obviously not hunting. It was as though he were reconnoitering to adjust his bearings. His fur was bright even in the shade, and he shone like a red coal when he flew through patches of sun. Being migratory, he had flown north, possibly from as far away as Central America; no definite information exists as to the exact limits of their long flights. Now, here he was, turning his head to look down as he circled. It was still a long way to the deep pine forests of New England and Canada—even to the fringes of the Arctic Circle—where he would breed and where his two young would first know true flight. He circled yet once more as I watched; then, as though to "shake down," he gave an abrupt, uneven series of flutters, left his circling pattern, and flew in a straight line directly into the north and disappeared.

Thinking of that Hoary bat and the mahogany color of his fur reminds me, as red-furred animals often do, that the Red squirrel is no longer in these woods. He was gone long before we came to live here thirteen years ago, driven out by the more blatant and less fastidious Grays. I did not use "blatant" only because I could not for the moment think of the word "aggressive." I used it because the smaller Red squirrel is actually the more aggressive, being able to put a Gray to flight if it feels in the mood. But though noisy and perpetually active, Red squirrels are less adapted than the parkside, peanut-eating, ubiquitous Grays. It is as though the Red squirrels just plainly had better taste and would not deign to stoop to the common level of the Grays. They were not "driven out," particularly; but rather, it would seem, simply "preferred to leave," having, in spite of a close and friendly enough association with humans, a basically feral attitude about them. And so, they have left. Preferring the seed-bearing cones of the conifers, Red squirrels are more plentiful in pine-woods areas; but in this region, too, they were once commonly found. Only fifteen or so miles to the southward, at the edge of the Pine Barrens, Red squirrels are still common. But not here. It is our loss.

There are some consolations in these woods, by way of at least partial compensation for the Red squirrel, and one is that the chipmunk is yet with us. Not that this is anything unusual. They are all over the East. Most commonly so. They are in every garden, perhaps, and sometimes a nuisance. But common or not, we are still thankful for them. I saw one today: he came out of the oak leaves, sat on a stump, and scolded me. Then he flicked his tail and ran away.

Late March is the first time it is possible to look at our estuary with even the slightest notion of ever actually being *in* it again, even in a boat. The hardy clam diggers and fishermen are used to the ice and winter's cold—but to anyone warmly shut in during the months of freezing weather, water in the open is a chill prospect.

But in March, particularly on warm, sunny days, for the first time there is a "smell" to everything. One's nose is at this time used consciously as a tool, as a device to detect the variegated essences loosed from the sterility of winter's grasp. Nearly everything wants sniffing at as March matures and begins to wane. Our Pandora's box contains the first spikes of skunk cabbage, the reek of loam, the now-not-unpleasant odor of a long-dead fish, the bark of a tree, a cedar branch brushed in passing, the salt dampness of an old catboat upturned for the first time since October. And above all, you can smell the tide.

April

In Memoriam

April. I scarcely believe I shall make it over the line! The night
of the thirty-first of March seems the longest of the year . . .
and then it is *April!*

Why make so great a thing of it? I cannot tell you, for April
is scarcely different from March, at least during the first weeks.
Often it is colder, rainier, more miserable. Sometimes there is
snow: a cold wet clog of slush, spattering, soiling, and undigni-
fied. But it never lasts. Nothing does in April. It is a month of
juggling about and straightening away.

> *April is the cruelest month,*
> *Breeding lilacs out of the dead land . . .*

Whatever it is that happens out of accord in winter's last throes,
soon it will be over. Winter chill, mud, gray skies, and weariness. Weariness of waiting. The first wild geese clanging up the
skies give notice. First they come in March, but in April one
sees them still: active, crying out, vibrant, alive. Ah, my good
geese! And there is not so much a sight of things, but a sign of
things. The first blades of real grass, the swelling of buds to near
bursting, the running of sap—all of it is just over the line. It all
began in March—but in March there was the long run from

February, the long run that would *never* end. But now it is the first of April. Why, it is really very nearly May! You see . . . April is not so much a month as an attitude of the mind.

"Spring peeper" is a childhood term common to children nearly anywhere but on the cement-bound city streets. Even there, the occasional damp lot or untended ditch may, in April, give forth a sweetness of sound more welcome, even, than that of still-arriving birds. Few need be told that our clarion peeper is a frog. Most of us, when young and in a fever to shake off winter's gray cloak, have been drawn by those sweet notes to places of cattails and marshy ground to try to "find the peeper." Perhaps we spent hours and never did find him. Or perhaps we persisted, scraping round through the fallen leaves and brown

rubble, until suddenly we cupped our hands over a little frog with a Saint Andrew's cross on his back. And perhaps, too—as have generations before—we put the wee creature into a jar to see him later puff out his tissue-thin throat and sing. And how he does sing! But the sound falls more sweetly on the ear when emanating from pondside or marsh.

The peeper is a *Hyla*, or tree frog (though he is generally on the ground). But April is the month of other frogs, as well. Having lain in a torpor over the winter, they are first wakened by the thin but warming rays of March's sun. In April they begin to thaw, and one can imagine them—unbearably stiff in their joints—creaking to a pool's edge to plop listlessly into the water, their arms and legs outstretched and their eyes half-closed, as though further effort were a thing too burdensome to bear. Then one foot might give a push and they would slowly drift to a mossy bank, there—half in and half out of the water—to lie in a cold-rubber state to slowly absorb the heat of the sun. I have often seen them so.

But soon the sun grows warmer; a few early insects begin to creep or, like the frogs, to stiffly try a few airborne flights. Perhaps in their lethargy they may miss their mark and land with a tiny splash and flutter near our comatose frog. This will awaken him. The stiffness will soon leave his joints and he will be actively engaged in shouting his love in a "froggie would a-wooing go" fashion, finding his mate, and getting into the great springtime activity of nature, that of procreation. Not long after there will be transparent, tapioca-like masses of eggs; then tiny tadpoles, older tadpoles, tadpole-like half-frogs, then new frogs, all jumping about and making a pleasant din.

There are more kinds of frogs than one might think. Though the peeper is often the first to sing, he is soon joined by the Green frog, Leopard frog, Pickerel frog, Cricket, Wood, and Bullfrogs. Each is strikingly patterned in cool, pleasant greens, yellows, grays and browns. Perhaps the tree frogs—particularly the Green Tree frog and Anderson's Tree frog—are the most

daintily sculptured and most attractive, but all of them are gracefully proportioned, pleasingly streamlined, and agile.

A favorite frog of mine is the Wood frog. He is one of the
first frogs active in the spring, and coinhabits the chilled pools
with the peeper. To the peeper's sweet whistle, the Wood frogs
add their "clack-clack," which often sounds like the quacking
of ducks. They are often found away from moist ground and
are dry (therefore pleasant to catch) rather than wet and
slippery. They are often the color of dried beech leaves and are
handsome with their unmarked backs and dark, broad eye-
stripes. How often have I caught them and "put them to sleep"
by turning them over and quietly and gently stroking their
stomachs; they become as pliable as though made of rubber,
sinking into a state of complete relaxation. When released,
they remain stupefied for long minutes; then, suddenly awake,
they will hop away.

Another favorite is the Cricket frog. He usually does not
begin to sing until late April or May, but then his "click-clack"
sound resembles the loud tin "crickets" which perennially accompany small boys.

Frog voices are seldom unpleasant in themselves (a receptive
state of mind, however, is often a prerequisite to enjoyment if
the ponds be close by). Like anything else—the cheery robin,
for instance, perched in bursting song outside the window at
five o'clock in the morning—frogs can be monotonous. The
"sleigh-bells" of the peepers, however, joined in chorus by the
Wood frog's "clack," and the baritone of the middle-sized frogs,
can be a smoothly soothing symphony. Especially toward the
end of April (when the peepers have long stopped) when the
basso profundo of the Bullfrog is heard, does one grow to appreciate frog voices. This giant among frogs (to upwards of 3
pounds) is rare in many places because the gastronomic delights
of its epicurean legs make it a target for market hunters. But in
our backwater they are plentiful, and their "jug-o-rum" re-
verberating in the scent-filled, late April dark is a lovely sound
indeed. On one occasion I came upon my own children—

ostensibly fishing for Small-mouthed bass in the ice pond—
actually catching Bullfrogs by dangling their (bassless) lures
under the side of the overhanging banks. Out would plummet
the great frogs to snare themselves on the wicked barbs. In being
called to witness this procedure, I was instructed (with just a
hint of defensive guilt, for they well knew how fishhooks felt
being extracted from themselves) that "lots of people eat them."
I replied that *I* ate them and that they could do what they liked
in the matter of frogs, but that I preferred to listen rather than
to eat. They pondered this, then decided it would be far less of
a world without old "jug-o-rum" and thereafter ceased their
torment. I vividly remember one they proudly showed me that
day, however; he was a brilliant emerald green and bright yellow, his great tympanic drum stood out, his belly was fat, his
skin smooth, and his eye was sparkling bright. What a great,
lovely monster he was! And how his progeny still boom from
the pond on April nights!

Toads are also in our woods, but not generally seen until
later on as spring matures. Toads are a sort of dry-land, nocturnal
"frog" with rough, warty skin (rather than smooth, as with
frogs). They "hop" slowly, rather than going about in frenetic
froglike leaps. They lay their eggs in long strings rather than
in masses, and quietly and harmlessly patrol the woodland,
ferreting under stones and logs to find insects. Their lovely soft
trill is one of the sweetest sounds of spring.

Also in April there is a general awakening of most cold-
blooded animals: salamanders, turtles, and snakes all begin to
come out of their winter slumbers and slowly take stock and, at
last, to move about more briskly. It takes *time* to thaw.

April eventually bursts into a cascade of green. Before that
explosive metamorphosis, however, the drab, colorless raiment
of winter often persistently clings until the month is well in the
wane. When this occurs, and if it should coincide with a dry
period of little snow or rain, here in New Jersey Robert Lewis
Stevenson's

Sing a song of seasons,
Something bright in all,
Flowers in the summer,
Fires in the fall . . .

is somewhat reversed. For spring fires are a great danger here before the moisture-laden, young green leaves put a mantle of dampness over last autumn's dried leaf cover. Generally such fires are started by young boys—for at this season no poachers come into the woods—or by a careless cigarette thrown from a passing car.

On one Palm Sunday not long ago, we had such a fire. It was started the day before by a cigarette, for the small blaze was at the edge of the road by the barn and was stoutly attacked in its infancy by Otto, a neighboring hired man, whose picturesque barrage of linguistic comment in German is one to incite wonder. With what shining vigor did Otto's rake beat out the flames! I had been summoned from the barn and was equally well employed in the rake-wielding and in the use, myself, of a rather sultry flow of idiomatic diversification. For fires bring out in one the vengeful spirit of aroused masculinity, attack seldom being so sanguine as in the face of holocaust. We put out the fire, and confined it to less than an acre in a wild, concentrated assault. When the fire department arrived they saw a very blackened and smoke-stained pair smugly surveying their conquest. The fire people gave it an extra lick with their light hose, just for good measure.

But neither measure was good enough. Sometime during the night a spark, hidden away in the dried root of some stump, grew in intensity to spread upward into a flame. Then a brisk wind off the sea caught the flame and fanned it into a roaring blaze. The blaze grew and raced up the hillside.

We were awakened by sirens in the dark hours of early morning. The woods were veiled in smoke, and the glow of the fire line was a jagged gash on the hillside, slowly burning toward us against the wind. All neighboring men were out with the fire volunteers, but little progress was possible against the wind. The fire raged all of that day. Women set up a canteen on our little lawn, from which came a perpetual flow of coffee and sandwiches to sustain the fire fighters. Our house was hosed down, as were several others in the surrounding countryside. But still the fire raged all around us. Other fire companies were called and came. Finally, a large bulldozer was employed to clear fire trails, and some headway was made. But the coming of evening brought a renewal of the stiff wind, which had died down during the day. All gains were soon lost, and it became a serious situation indeed. Dead trees glowed like torches even after the fire was well past, and the wind caught at the live flames and flung them high into the air to infect yet another area with fire. The smoke was choking, and everyone was blackened and bone-weary, but still no efforts were slackened. The ground was extremely dry, and the compost had dried into hard cakes of peat which defied all efforts to extinguish them.

For yet another day and night the fire continued; now raging, now nearly out—then starting up again with renewed ferocity. Finally, a change in wind plus a light rain did at last put out the last vestiges of flame. Smoke lingered, however, for many days.

Who can tell how many small lives were lost in that fire? I found rabbits burned to death in their holes; mice and squirrels were incinerated by hundreds; birds fared better, but dead birds were found. Every living thing was affected, from earthworms and wood lice and beetles to foxes, raccoons, and skunks. And yet, at summer's height, little was to be seen even of scars, and the loss of animal life seemed to have virtually no effect on the wild population. And yet there was surely loss. How many tragedies were played out cannot be guessed.

Those infernal, DAMNED foxes! Now what else can I say? They have killed my goose. My good, peaceable, warm-natured, really quite lovable goose. Dead now. Inert. Buried under the roots of some hollies just below the big spruce. How she would "talk" to me. "Good morning, Goose," I would shout, and she would unfailingly answer with a cascade of honest sound, cocking her head and giving me a quizzical look. Her burial was attended by five children. One was aloof. One was sober. One cried (but more in keeping with the occasion than in obdurate sorrow). One—very small—was eminently practical, though unconcerned about the trivialities of gender, when he said, "The old goose is dead. He'll smell if we don't bury him." And the fifth "child" was very tall—myself. I was silent, but I was mentally damning every protective Saint of Animals ever etched on a bronze door or painted on a triptych—and, I'm afraid, throwing an extra curse or two particularly in the direction of St. Francis. "Might have been more on the job," I fumed. But it was no slipshod shepherding on anyone else's part. The door to the fowl yard had carelessly been left ajar, and the old goose had walked out in the very early morning—still "fox time." And she had been killed by a quick, cruel, wrenching grasp of jaws on her poor head. But she was heavy, and the fox had been small or, possibly, not adept at slinging a goose over his shoulder (as they have been known to do). We found her, uneaten, dragged halfway up the hillside. I was very much saddened and couldn't help uttering a final "Good morning, Goose," as we covered her with warm earth.

It may begin to seem that each sequence of events retold here ends in death, and perhaps you may think this chronicle has taken on a moribund flavor. It is not that. It is that long association with any wild creatures—their lives, generally, are much shorter than ours—will, if their story be fully told, end in death. Seldom does a wild animal die peaceably abed. Death is certain for wild things, but it is not always a tragedy. My old goose was taken by a fox; a good, honest end. Far better an end than the oily pavement under the wheels of a car. I am furious with the fox, for it is only human to be so, but I feel no enmity. And I am deeply convinced that the gentle saint who preached to the birds is not really falling down on his heavenly job. To circumambulate the ending in a natural tale is either to dismiss reality or to employ the cowardly literary device of feigning ignorance. The first is childish, the last is despicable. Either is an insult to intelligence.

And so, my old goose is gone. And we buried her.

This subject has been—until recently—the focal point of our lives. The subject is eagles. Not at all does it concern eagles in general, but "our own" eagles. Yes, to these we lay claim—that is, as we might "claim" any wild thing. For, until only a very few years ago (to be exact, 1962) a pair of Bald eagles—that noble raptor depicted in our national emblem—nested each year in a very tall oak scarcely more than a hundred yards from our back door. It sounds ridiculous to speak of Bald eagles nesting "in our back yard" but this was actually the case, for the property rises over the hill behind the house and opens out into a field, then down to the water. In between lies a deep gully, the road, and then another hill in front. In a way, it is as though the higher hills were in the form of a backwards question mark, with the house cradled in the closed end and the point and dot opening out into the barn and cove. The eagles' nest rose high above the hill on which it stood, commanding as enviable an aspect of sea, estuary, hills, and woodland as one could desire.

A good friend of some years, older than I, told me that the eagles' nest was there on the hill when she was a girl, well over fifty years ago; and, since the family has been in residence here continuously, both before and since that time, it is of definite record that the eagles, too, have been constant in their residency during that time. Although eagles are known to possess a long life span, it is not likely that the same pair inhabited the nest during that period; but it is most likely that successive generations of the same eagle family did carry on the occupancy. Thus, the family of eagles nesting here (not necessarily in the exact nest, but close in proximity) were a lineage long established and venerable and a strong stock, as would befit eagles.

When we came to live here it took a good while getting used

to eagles so close by, and it took the eagles a longer time to get used to us. At first, though we had been told of their presence and sworn to protect them, we actually saw little of them. But as time went on, the great birds seemed gradually to become used to us; they became less just distant objects and took on form and identity as they cautiously edged ever nearer. It must, indeed, have been a bother to fly in circuitous detours simply to bypass a tiny human far below. Finally, we were evidently exonerated from suspicion, for one day an eagle appeared on the limb of a nearby oak. At such close range the bird looked to us more the size of the legendary Roc: it seemed gigantic! Admonishing each other not to "look up" but to go quietly about whatever we were doing, we could not help but notice we were being given the "acid test." And we passed—for after a time we saw (out of the corners of our eyes) that the giant bird had jumped to another branch and had, in seeming disdain, turned its back to us and was idly preening its feathers. After that time they seemed to come as close as they chose—often to fly into a tree directly above our heads.

Their old nest was of an enormous size—as large nearly as our kitchen floor. It was a very large platform indeed—though this kind of computing is really of little value unless accurate measurements are made. And we seldom ventured close enough to the nest for actual measurement for fear of losing our status of "harmless." Only once, actually, did we climb a nearby tree to pry into their business, and that was when we suspected something had happened to the newly hatched young. Even then we had a chain of children strung out to give warning of their return from the tidal flats. We saw little, as it turned out, for the eagles had the highest tree around, and vertigo was our only reward for climbing the adjacent tree. It was a useless expedition anyway, for the young eagles had merely been younger than we thought, and soon appeared at the edge of the nest. As they matured, their down could be seen wafting through the branches and trees below.

The nest itself was not by any means a flat platform, but had

been begun in a high fork and built upwards; the result being a long wedge, much like an ice cream cone licked flat on top. It stood not on the top but on the side of the hill, in a truly giant Black oak—an oak so large that, as I say, it rose above even the Chestnut oaks, an unmixed stand of which graced the top of the ridge. Only a trident of large dead limbs, virtually branchless and bleached white, rose above the nest itself; they were at an angle too steep for sitting upon, so the eagles flew always to the nest itself. The vista that nest commanded was such that it must have given the keen-sighted birds a minute-by-minute chronicle of any event unfolding below. One of our children, in being taken to the crest of the hill to be shown the eagles' domain and told of the bird's powers of vision, asked, "Could he tell if a mouse sneezed?" And I answered that it seemed not unlikely.

It was a thing of which we were never fully certain, of course, but it seemed that our position of coexistent harmony within the eagles' domain extended also to the other animals. Never once in all of the hundreds of times eagles came to roost near the house was even the vaguest hint given by the great birds that they coveted what was ours. Our chickens and ducks waddled and quacked and clucked directly under the eagles. Although the goose never failed to keep a beady eye riveted on the eagle, the lesser fowls seemed not to take notice—and, on the eagle's part, though he (or she) often spent hours looking down on that scene of barnyard bliss, it was never with that raptorial eagerness so well known to anyone cognizant of eagles, but with a sort of vague bemusement or (less anthropomorphically) a tolerant benignity. We were given every reason to believe that no "local" animals, under whatever bounds set by themselves as *le droit du seigneur*, were ever touched or molested. Rabbits and squirrels, that "froze" whenever certain hawks came near, seemed to go about in an ordinary fashion in this eagledom, as though assured of sanctuary. Now this—I have to suspect—may be a pure fabrication of humanized nonsense, and I tell you so plainly. But still I can only describe what I

have seen and noted. Within the so-called protectorate or, orni-
thologically speaking, "territory" of the eagles, there did *seem*
to be that aura of sanctuary. I can guarantee nothing. But such
is what we saw.

As years passed, young eagles survived, matured into the
first- and second-year plumage of uniform sepia brown, then
gloriously appeared (it can be supposed) sometime in the third
year in the adult full dress of white head and white tail. I say "it
can be supposed" for, at home, we only saw two (presumably
the same) adults year in and year out. The young ones all
seemed to leave. There was (then) another nest off beyond
McClee's Creek and another down toward Little Silver. "Our"
birds seemed to stick tight—going off (somewhere) for a few
months during the winter, but generally being around at most
times, sitting on the ice eating a fish, sailing like a flat, dark
shingle over the azure sky of May, or shaking away August's
dew in the gnarled tree over the causeway.

With the very few individuals who lived in our treasured
little hollow the eagles, then, became a fixture. We grew to
accept their presence with a naïveté which now (and this is but
a very few years later) seems hopelessly puerile. Might not so
much more have been done to record this intimate relationship
only scant miles from populous New York? Not really. The
scientifically astute National Audubon Society was aware of
the nest and its occupants, and we were jointly concerned only
with keeping the eagles' presence a quiet secret, not with flam-
boyantly plastering it into headlines. Our *sub rosa* devices—not
to mention the sympathetic support of the local populace—kept
the nest operative and lent it protection from any outside in-
fluences. I still insist it was a puerile concept, however—our
"taking it all for granted." Could you but see *now* the vista
from that height of land! Now there are a cluster of $60,000
(and upwards) houses not far from the nest site, colored all
in pink and blue and green. Eagles, now, would seem out of
place.

But *then*—say, in the mid-fifties—the eagles were surely a

common everyday thing with us. As I would walk each morning
to the barn before the sun rose, when just a bare light would be
showing through the trees in the east; when still the stars were
clearly discernible and objects were not always easily picked
out; when my dog, still, might stumble over a stone, and footfalls
of both dog and man were more readily heard because many
birds had not yet joined in the dawn chorus—these times the
eagle could often be seen skulking along the trees above the
road . . . doing what, at that hour, I cannot imagine. There was
a favorite perch along the causeway, as I have said. One morning,
enveloped by the faintest aura of rose as the sun came up, I
sat quietly near that perch after the eagle (one of them, I could
not tell which) had flown there after an early bath. The shining
spray of droplets shaken from his (or her) feathers made a
delicate rainbow as they were flung into a halo. On that morning
the white head feathers pin-pointed themselves so that the
eagle's head seemed a hedgehog of tiny white spikes, until a
few more vigorous shakes had dried them and they began to lie
flat. How he shone in the immaculate whiteness of that head!
Once during this operation, as I moved slightly to admire the
sun rising over the water, he cast down a long, thoughtful glance
—not sideways in bird fashion, but straight down around his
glistening yellow beak, like a staid librarian suddenly confronted
by a small boy holding a badly torn book. Then he resumed
his preening. I sat for nearly an hour under that tree, letting the
essence of that scene etch itself deeply into my consciousness;
not consciously registering the depths of my appreciation, but
somehow letting the acid of that regal loveliness penetrate into
my soul. But then! . . . I know nothing of souls—my own or
anyone else's . . . and should not go round blathering about them.

At other times we (and by "we" I mean not only myself
and my possibly impressionable family, but a round half-dozen
of respectable and sober neighbors, whose word would be inviolate . . . a thing I did take into consideration before divulging
all this) would watch the eagles robbing the ospreys on the
"stage" of ether above the tidal flats. I remember one incident

when an osprey was flying, in obvious labor, with a really very large fish—the tail of which kept slowly flapping and from which water still dripped. The osprey saw the descent of the eagles and started screaming, still clutching the fish and pumping its long wings in a propulsive burst of energy. But to no avail—the eagles raked the osprey, who, in turning over, dropped the fish from a height of 30 feet. It plopped into the mud below as the osprey (cursing shrilly) side-slipped out from under while the eagles dropped down to make off with their plunder. I remember this so vividly because during all this rather dramatic goings-on, clearly in view of everyone on the terrace of the house which overlooks the cove, one of the guests, while watching the birds, poured himself another long gin and tonic, and never once stopped talking of the Bermuda Race. Then, when the drama was over and the fish had been borne skyward by the eagles, he said, "Eagles must make a funny footprint in the mud with all that great length of claws. . . ." I stopped to marvel; for I saw that beneath the drone of talk about coffee-grinder winches, depth indicators, and Ratsey's latest threading device lay the workings of a very versatile and agile mind, and that his appreciation was as deep as my own.

At yet another time we were all gathered on the long screened verandah of R.B.'s house, which overlooks the pond. (I would have said "having cocktails"—which we were—but such a bare-faced revelation might not, I quickly considered, lend credence to this precisely stated and accurate anecdote. That is what we were doing, anyway: having cocktails.) As we were all trading local banter—it was an enchanted, calm Sunday afternoon in late May—of rose pruning, raspberry plantings, 5-10-5 versus 10-10-10 (or whatever combinations of organics they were), our attention was called to two Snowy egrets and some Painted turtles that had arranged themselves on a half-submerged log lying in the pond. We stopped talking to admire the egrets and listen to R.B. explain that although the Painted turtles were all right, the Snapping turtles, he was certain, were taking young ducks. As we watched, an eagle slowly spiralled down to alight on the same great, barkless gray-brown log that held the egrets. Not one of us took a breath—for neither egret nor turtles moved. The eagle leisurely drank and had a good long preen before he flapped away—leaving the egrets (and R.B.'s young ducklings) still standing there. We—all of us—carefully explored each other's faces for some hint of alcohol-induced madness, but we were as clear-eyed and as sober as any but the most vicious of abstentious critics could demand. The thing had happened. As simply as though with cut-out birds in a pie-dish pond. Later one of the egrets left too, his white reflection mirrored in the water as he flew over the pond. We were adult and far from irresponsible, I believe; and one of us, I can promise you, drank only ginger ale. And the eagle did come, and did exactly as I have said.

It was an odd thing, but the greatly relaxed familiarity displayed by our eagles seemed most strictly rationed. I was among those honored, as were my wife, my children, and my dog. Six or seven others, including Holmes Crawford, who cut the large lawns with a great, thrashing piece of sit-down machinery, were also "in the Club." I could walk down the road with my dog and go directly under the eagles sitting above. Should I have stopped, of course, and made loud shouting noises—as I had with the Horned owls—the eagles would quickly have flown off. But we were all most wary about taking liberties, even the children. It was possible, even, to approach them across an open field, coming quite close to the tree in which they sat. Too obvious a detour, however, out of that which they considered a reasonable terrestrial trajectory, would cause a cautious exit through the surrounding trees. It always amazed me how such great birds *could* go through trees at all—but actually, of course, they usually just swept low and appeared to be among the branches. But all of this friendly camaraderie would vanish in an instant if only one foreign element be stirred in as an ingredient. For instance, were a visiting friend to join me as I walked homeward with my dog, the same eagle who would at every other time be sitting close by would keep to a wide perimeter, nearly out of sight. Or even, were that friend's small and decidedly harmless dog in evidence in the yard, no eagle would come near. After becoming aware of this, we began to test the premise. I would walk, for example, past a roosting eagle. Then I would walk back again. The eagle took little notice. One more time I would do this, and repeat the return. The same result. Then, another party, waiting in concealment, would join me at the same pace. The eagle's reaction was first to look hard, then to crane forward as though for a better look; finally he would silently glide off and be gone. Time after time did we work our little experiment, and inevitably the result was the same. I am in no position to say that this is a usual reaction—or even if there might not have been an omission on my part which might well invalidate any genuine conclusion. It was not a truly scientific experiment, but really more of a game.

The eagles are dead, of course. Whatever of natural things may one day be coaxed back into some new kind of Eden brought about by compromise, the eagles will not be among them. They were shot; first one, then the other. They died not so much by the hand of any single young culprit, as by the ignorance of "country" values which accompanies the growth of houses toadstooling in our woods. But it is not "our" woods—it is theirs too. Later, it will be they who will take up the cry of havoc in our midst. In the meanwhile, starling minds and starling manners prevail. Eagles are forever gone from this place, the last area in sight of New York City.

Might not the eagles have gone anyway? Yes, for during the last three years before their extermination, they brought forth no young. Their eggs, it is said, were sterile. Whatever the cause —insecticides or some reason yet unknown—Bald eagles are in retreat throughout the East. Where there will be a final stand is a matter of question.

It was always easy to identify our eagles in flight, even when their white heads and tails were blended into a milky background of sky. It was not only their size, for size can be deceptive. Nor was it any lumbering quality, suggestive of great bulk—which, of course, they did possess. Rather, it was the more rigid plane of their wings and a certain aspect of, perhaps, controlled weight. They "sailed" across the sky. The majesty felt in seeing their starkly contrasting plumage against the sky was, of course, not without extraneous connotations—inclusive of everything from patriotism, through history and heraldry, down to multiply-diverse concepts in art. But "majesty" is not easily defined: it is a positive quality either present or totally lacking. One can never be half-majestic. Majesty is "holding sway," ruling in dignity, with the full authority of sovereign power. An eagle is somehow possessed of this rare quality even when standing in the mud with soiled feathers and eating a disgusting morsel of carrion. . . . All of this, however, is a purely personal, not at all scientific, and—very possibly—not very accurate description. Benjamin Franklin once vehemently opposed the Bald eagle as an inferior carrion-eater and plumped vigorously for the adoption of the Wild turkey as national symbol in its stead. Witmer Stone, a distinguished ornithologist, has called this eagle "a degenerate member of the eagle tribe whose whole life and character have been modified by a fish diet." All of which is true. I maintain, however, that majesty and bearing and the power to stir men's minds are qualities which rise above minor weaknesses and vagaries of appetite. The flight of eagles *commands* attention, as does a meteorite's plunge . . . and many of us might wish to echo the words of Thomas Merton: "I wonder if my admiration for you gives me an affinity for you, artist! I wonder if there will ever be something connatural between us, between your flight and my heart stirred in hiding, to serve Christ, as you, soldier, serve your nature."

May

Of Bogs and Meadow Mice

In every May, with the same beauty of sight and sound, we do beget that golden time again. VISCOUNT GREY OF FALLODON

Trailing arbutus is a most delicate and delightful plant. It grows low to the ground—literally *on* the ground—and its white, blended-with-pink flowers are fragrantly and exquisitely fragile. So, when not many days ago my wife, in walking across our lawn down the path toward the log cabin (there is one, deep in a hollow behind our house), came upon three gross and sweating women busily employed tearing up great sections of one of our favorite beds, she was, to say the least, wild. On top of that there were three or four scruffy children squatting and stamping and pulling arbutus up by the handful. I am sorry to say that on neither side of the exchange was there anything like dulcet tones of apology or gentle admonitions to desist. Barbara's demeanor at all times—give or take a few widely separated instances such as the children's drowning *The New York Times Book Review* in the duck pond or some equally horrendous act —is reasonably gracious and proper; not cloying, mind you, just proper. But this situation was enough to snap the strongest reserve: one of the great, fat oafs was even crushing, as she yanked away, a yard-wide area of flowers with the seat of her dress—if that is the correct term. Barbara's rage was demoniac; she shrilled like a fishwife, threatening to call me, the police, the governor (in that order, I am pleased to report), for I overheard it all on my way to the back lawn to see what unearthly row this was. The others used nasty language at first, and then began to whine in a most contemptible fashion—their excuse being that they had "always picked flowers here."

"Picking flowers, indeed," said Barbara. "You're *destroying* them—so get out." And they got out.

I certainly didn't help matters any by bowing low and inquiring, "Can I be of service, ladies?"

"Ladies!" snorted Barbara, urging them on with the point of a walking stick, and giving me a look that would kill.

Some time later—that evening, I remember—as Barbara was checking Theodore Bernstein on the obscure distinction between "synechdoche" and "metonymy" and running on in an aside to one of the children, in general about rhetorical figures, she suddenly stopped and looked up at some of the crushed arbutus she had gathered into a little crystal glass. "Wretched, miserable," I heard her mutter.

I asked, "Did I hear you correctly?"

"Yes, you did," she answered.

"Not very charitable—couldn't you have cut a wider swath calling them 'paronomasia' or 'onomatopoeia?'" I replied. "Or how about an oxymoron?"

"I don't think you're so funny," she said, still smarting. "They had no right to tear them up that way."

The moral here is that if you walk in a patch of woods and stop to admire arbutus, make certain that you not only know "meiosis" botanically as well as rhetorically, but that you don't confuse "hypocotl" with "hyberbole"—for if you should, Mr. Bernstein wouldn't get you out of that one, and on top of it, it might be poison ivy. Oh yes, and Trailing arbutus is in bloom now. Just outside and across the lawn. Under the oaks.

Today I saw the last remaining blooms of the Dog-toothed violets. These were but a freakish holdover, however, for the sturdy little lilies ordinarily reach their peak here in April. It was in a dark, cool hollow at the head of the gully that I found these few recalcitrant yellow flowers. Their twin-bladed, darkly mottled leaves, and erect stature, were as firm as though it were early last month and not mid-May. Also called the Yellow Adder's Tongue, their soft yellow flowers often cover square yards of shaded brookside. And I should indeed have come to mention this boyhood favorite of mine before now had I not, in April, been either irascibly condemning or extolling (no doubt with violent gestures of punctuation) something else. Nature, too, is seldom neutral. There is either peace or fury; gray passivity is rare. The sight of this quiet flower of early spring means much to me—but you must follow it into regions of moist

banks and swampy places and, this year, I nearly missed seeing it.

Another flower of earlier spring is the Spring Beauty, *Claytonia virginica*. It is a most delicate and sweet-scented member of the Purslane family, a Portulaca. No boy who is country-bred has not got down on grubby knees to smell them and to bear them proudly home in a soiled warm fist—they wilting with every step. The flower is "white"—but seldom is, being nearly always flushed with a crimson-pink issuing from a pale yellow base. The flower has but five fragile petals, and its undulating stem and narrow leaves are equally tender. Also a lover of open, moist woods, this lovely plant is often found side by side with the Dog-toothed violet. The Spring Beauty, however, is usually first to bloom and is usually on the wane when the "violets" appear. This year I failed to see either in its proper time and now, for this flower, the time is far past.

A heron at rest always seems more reptile than bird. The long, supple neck and the staring yellow eye is disconcerting; even the feathers are slicked down and tightly locked into an armor plate. Only in the spring, when their plumes are waving and surround them like a fine spray, does the sitting bird take on any true appeal.

But a heron in flight is far different. Even then they are inclined toward a jerkiness in movement when rising or alighting, and in full flight they often appear to labor. But the effect is always of grace and languidness, as though the world might hurry, but not they. Their slow flight mirrored in a still pond has all the quality of peace and serenity that one sees in Japanese prints—such prints, in fact, as often as not depicting the graceful heron.

One most obvious is the American egret. He is entirely white with a yellow bill and black legs, and stands motionless for long periods waiting to strike at his prey. He wears long "aigrettes," or plumes, during breeding season, which droop gracefully from his back. This egret returns from the south rather early and is fairly common in and around our pond. The Snowy egret is smaller, also white, but with a sharp black bill and black legs. His feet, though, are bright lemon yellow, as though he had pulled on yellow socks. This beautiful bird carries plumes on both head and back. Both egrets now commonly breed in the trees nearby, and there is a large rookery on Sandy Hook.

We also have in evidence the Little Blue heron, which before it matures is white; and the African Cattle egret is an occasional visitor. The American Bittern skulks in the salt marsh below the gully; and the small "Shite-poke," the Little Green heron, solemnly plods the pond edge or, with far more rapid wing-beats than most herons, flies quickly from dead tree stump to marsh fringe—always prodding and prying. The tiny Least bittern has never shown himself in our marsh—but then, he is very small and easily overlooked.

The most vocal of these stilt-fishermen is the Black-crowned night heron, whose "quok, quok" is a familiar sound during late spring evenings. The Yellow-crowned night heron has been seen nearby but not by me.

The largest and perhaps best known of all our local herons is the Great Blue. He always seems even larger than he is—and is large enough at that. His pale gray body, russet wrist and leg feathers; his white head and swept-back ear-crest; his long stilt legs and stout, sharp bill; and his glassy, piercing eye—all combine to lend an aura of grandfatherly dignity and an Edwardian hauteur to this great marsh bird. He, like the American egret, waits silently, or patrols the shallows with great patience; then, in a lightning stroke, transfixes some hapless marine animal with his rapier bill. Once, in South Carolina, I watched Great Blue herons (and American egrets as well) patrolling the far edge of a section of salt marsh that was being burned over. Frantically trying to escape the flames were great numbers of the Rice rat, *Oryzomys palustris*, running blindly in every direction. As they rushed the gantlet of herons, many were pierced, lifted, and quickly swallowed. I remember it with intense clarity, for in more than one instance the thrashing animal was swallowed alive and one could clearly see its passage downward in the elastic gullet of the heron neck, swinging and kicking all the way down. Certainly one or two must have been biting as well, for they were hastily regurgitated, re-stabbed, then swallowed again. I made certain of my identification of the rats by chasing some herons after they had stabbed their rats and before they had a chance to swallow them. And they were—as I might add—fully grown Rice rats, not young ones. (The Rice rat is a medium-sized animal of southern distribution—reaching only part way up coastal New Jersey at its most northerly penetration.) The herons, speaking yet of the rat-catching incident, gorged until many could scarcely fly; one, at least, was so full of rats that in attempting to be airborne, he lost altitude and crashed ignominiously into the marsh grass.

Our own herons, here, also spear mice and smaller rats from time to time, but their general prey consists of frogs, tadpoles, fishes, and other aquatic life. Clams are often stabbed before they can completely close their shells, and a wrestling match evolves between heron and clam. Whatever it is they feed upon, they are regarded by us all as favorites among our common birds. It is always a pleasure to see their slow wing-beats across the evening sky, their necks tucked up and back, their great legs trailing, and their steady, purposeful flight leading upward into the gloom of night's descent. We know they will return tomorrow.

Hawks are not common here any longer. They have been decreasing ever since we came here, thirteen years ago. During migration, of course, we have all sorts of birds of prey come effortlessly through on set wings or pause to "mill" high above in the thermal currents generated by our (humble, but adequate) hills. The Red-tailed hawk is with us permanently and nests near the radar station. The Red-shouldered hawk is sometimes here, but more often is not. The Cooper's hawk used to be here, but is no longer. Only the little Kestrel is, hawkwise, really very obvious at all. One pair nested this time last year in the old dead stub of an apple tree on the edge of the orchard. There was an ancient flicker hole nearby, but for two years there had been no occupant (other than, possibly, a White-footed mouse). I had come to think there was a flaw of some sort in the nesting cavity and that it would never be used again. But one day, there were the Kestrels.

Now Kestrels were called, in my youth—and even today— Sparrow hawks. They are not—that is, they seldom ever feed upon sparrows. And besides, there is a proper Sparrow hawk in England and Europe, an Accipiter (a *kind* of low-flying hawk). Also in England and on the continent is the Kestrel, a bird like our own but from which ours differs in minor points. Essentially, they are the same bird. And this gobbledygook of duplicity and cross and counter-duplicity in names is the result of early ignorance or of error. The sooner this situation gets itself straightened out by some hot-eyed revisionist, the better. Of course, much has already been done—and such actions will accelerate as greater travel and interchange continues to develop between this country and the womb of Europe from which we all sprang. Our Pigeon hawk (also a true falcon, as is our Kestrel) is really the Merlin of Europe, and has nothing whatever to do with eating pigeons—as his name is often construed to mean, though the bird is roughly of pigeon size.

At any rate, the Kestrels which nested in our old stub were as secretive a crew as could be imagined. You know how in open spaces these birds are clearly perched on some tall post or wire —well, in our woods they skulked in and out of that hole like criminals. That is, they behaved in that fashion as long as the eggs were unhatched. With young birds in the nest there was more of a bustle of activity. But as the young birds matured and flight training began, there seemed to be a happy hum over all of the orchard and a cartwheeling of Kestrels everywhere at once. They lost their former reticence and sat on the hay hoist, on the brass weathervane, and even came to sit where they could peer in at me working inside. They had a "training program" at the other end of the orchard; I could see the mother falcon hold- ing classes in the lower branches of the apple trees.

It is a pity that the full force of warbler migration just missed the investiture of the new leaves. For, once unfurled, the vestments of yellow-green at once begin to hide these small birds, themselves so brightly bedecked in spring plumage. I have been able to identify many in their southward autumnal flight as, dressed soberly as any monk, they filter through the baring trees and are away. But in spring they go through the woods like lighted sparks, their varieties many, their songs sweet, and their presence valued. Some stay to nest—others, more hyperborean, fly to the cold Canadian forests.

Our wood warblers are entirely different from the European warblers. They are of the Family *Parulidae*, all smaller than sparrows (with one exception, the Yellow-breasted chat); they have thin bills, bright colors, are extremely active, and feed upon insects. In the autumn, as I have indicated, they molt into drab plumage and do not change until the following spring when they return from the tropical south. Basically, they can be divided for purposes of identification into two: those with and those without "wing bars." That is, their shoulder feathers have white tips—thus "bars" when the wings are closed. Some of these birds are dull or at least olive-colored even in the spring, but all are beautifully sculptured and suggestive of speed and lightness.

It would be a redundancy to carefully list each species which flies through our woods, for they all do—twice each year. That is, those do which nest this far north—which is most of them. My favorites among them are the Chestnut-sided, Bay-breasted, Black-throated blue, Blackburnian, Parula, and Cape May. There is no special reason for my choices. Just color and association, probably. The Northern Yellow-throat and the Redstarts nest in the woods and are very common. The ground-haunting Ovenbird, with his stately walk and "oven" nest, soberly pokes round our lawn all summer long, as casually as any sparrow. His loud "teacher, teacher" call is as familiar as the children's voices. Both Water thrushes haunt our shaded glens during migration, and the Louisiana nests in the gully.

There are still some old-time, all-around "naturalists" left, it is said; those of the "Thoreau-Burroughs caliber." If there are, however, I cannot name them. Such a statement might well initiate a flood of objections, each loyally touting a candidate. But far from suggesting that there are not hundreds of well-informed individuals, each of whom may be widely versed in many categories of natural history, I say only that no single person can absorb the knowledge now amassed in the field. Seventy or a hundred years ago, one might nearly have. But knowledge has mushroomed and scattered its spores into so many diverse crevices of specialization that today one is fortunate in being able to grasp even a major portion of any single, isolated field of enquiry. How ridiculously quaint are many bird and flower books of even fifty short years ago! How naïve and how elementary! And yet—often—how charming they were, and (as often) how wise! There is no doubting that our massive output today in books and in disseminated knowledge is grand and impressive and immeasurably good (much of it, that is), but often we wallow so before the antiseptic altars of new gods of Science that perspective and depth are reduced to minimal entities which, at times, even disappear. In days past, Science was either "right" or "wrong." Now there exists the right, the wrong, and yet another, the pseudo-Science lying in between: a world of sterile half-truths and lackluster disclosures nearly always promoted for naked profit.

My saying all this, now, as I am engaged in describing to you the occupants and terrain of this far corner of what is really metropolitan New York City, is not to defend my own knowledge of this area or of the wild things contained in its protective woods, but rather to cast some doubt on the terms "expert" and "authority" which are now so liberally bestowed on anyone purporting to speak out in these times. It is as though a moving mouth were the only prerequisite to knighthood. There are indeed experts, however, here in New Jersey. W. Irving Black, James Lee Edwards, and Floyd Wolfarth are but a few. I remember the glowing fountains that were the late naturalists J. Fletcher Street, Charles A. Urner, and William J. Rusling. My own exploratory meanderings, even a few feet from my doorstep, are still accompanied by Roger Tory Peterson's indispensable *Field Guide to the Birds*, by an insect guide, and a pocket guide to flowers. I tell you this for I have just returned from Jack's gully and am sitting in a mood of frustration and anger as I quietly contemplate the enormity of what I do not know. I am at the moment smarting under my ignorance of botany, and my complete inability to describe accurately to you the plants with which I have lived now for many years. My mood of despair is not one of self-depreciation or quiescent inferiority —I can tell you, with regret, that I am often as stuffed full of pride as is an assemblage of minor politicians—but "Science" you see, is "to know"; half-knowing is unbearable. "Thinking" that you know is particularly galling, for seeds of doubt fast germinate into frustration. I sat there not half an hour ago, more in than out of a muddied pool at the side of our little stream. I had three reference books lying in the verdant leaves of the surrounding plants, each with a small stone to keep the pages from flapping. It was, I'll admit, a most obscure little fernlike plant whose identity I sought—and it was a young plant, besides. I poked and prodded and dug it up by the roots, but I could not discover even remotely what it was. I looked up into the blue May sky and cried out in exasperation, "Oh, if only I had Dave Fables now!" David Fables is dead, but he would have known that New Jersey plant. Of course, I shall find out what it is, but it will take time; and time enough is what none of us have. There is too much, far too much of everything else.

Jack's gully is not a name, really—it is only a gully that belongs to Jack. It is quite deep, cut by our very small stream of sweet, fresh water. Rich, black loam lines its sides, in which violets grow nearly 2 feet high and False Solomon's Seal reaches gigantic proportions. The high banks are filled with holly and immense tulip poplars that keep the gully in a damp shade, but —like a diminutive Grand Canyon—it is always warm in its deepest part, out of the wind, quiet and serene. The stream opens out into the salt marsh. Here grow the only trilliums to be found in our woods; the Wake Robin is the first, the Painted and Nodding trilliums follow. The Canada Mayflower, the Bellwort, and the Indian cucumbers are abundant. The Bloodroot, with its fragile petals of purest white, is commonly found on the banks. The Wood anemone and the even-lovelier Rue anemone are both here, as is the earlier Hepatica or Liverwort. The wild geranium's delicate blooms often cast a pale purple haze over our gully's crest, so thickly clustered are they there. And the May Apple or Mandrake is abundantly dispersed, again, on the higher slopes. These are all common flowers—it is for this reason that I know them, being, as I say, no botanist but only one who loves wildflowers. Much of my emotional appreciation, I realize, stems from a boyhood filled with these very things; but the even deeper appreciation springs from manhood's realization that such tender plants are becoming more and more rarely found by boys today.

There are no orchids in the gully for some reason unknown to me—for it seems as though orchids might be found there. We do have some orchids, however. Further up the hillside in an area of acid soil and Mountain laurel in unimaginably rich abundance (also thickly carpeted with shoulder-high wild azalea), the pink Lady's-slipper or Moccasin flower is not uncommon. I annually give thanks for its relative abundance; and its rare quality of simply *being* an orchid brings an exotic aura to our woods. The small, militarily stacked, creamy-white Rattlesnake plantain, another curious orchid with variegate leaves, does not bloom until later but is also common on the hillsides under the oaks. In only one spot—on a dry bank next to the large open field—does the Ladies' tresses grow, blooming only in late August or September. These are all our local orchids: a scant handful. The Yellow Lady's-slipper used to grow here in another large gully down closer to Rocky Point, but was bulldozed out to make way for new houses.

I might well go on, all in a litany (which Barbara and Bernstein both insist is the wrong usage of the word) about the many

wildflowers found here. They are manifold, prosperous, and
lovely. But nothing out of the ordinary. I tell you only of those
which are so commonly found that the younger children are
always filing in and out with tall jars of water filled with a pot-
pourri of them. Among flowers I am a child as well, and I return from the field, swamp, and woodland with my treasures,
each to be painstakingly identified and lovingly remembered.
But it does not last, however, this careful inspection of kinds.
Soon the abundance of flowers is overlaid with an equal abundance of birds, or of insects, or what-have-you, as springtime
leaps forward into high gear. Before long, detailed enquiry fades
into a blend—a whirl—of color and sound and scents, each more
poignant, more sweet, or more clarion than the last; and the
mind subsides into a stupor as summer approaches and ladles heat
over the warmth of spring.

I have somehow allowed myself to fall away from my own
(few) fields of any substantial knowledge. But flowers and
plants are an opiate to me in spring. It is time I returned to something about which I am more personally cognizant—yet I do not
wish to omit any subject which is, here, of local importance. So I
persist in a continual reiteration of my ignorance, which is embarrassing, but even at that, is better than a pose. In this case,
in some notes put aside, I wrote, "Bogs are different from swamps
and marshes." They are very different; but here, again, I am
plainly up against "scientific nomenclature" devised by ecolo-
gists. As deeply in love with natural things as I am, I am equally
in love with the English language. It is as splendid a vehicle for
description as Italian is for emotion and French for the subtly
obscure. English (at least as it was at its height and not as it
appears in retrogressive abuse) is as pointedly apt and lucid in
description as any language ever devised. Thus, in speaking of
bogs as opposed to swamps and marshes, I might not only compare each with the other, but, also, with morass, fen, slough,
quagmire, or water meadow. Then each could be subjugated by
such prefixes as fresh-, salt-, peat-, sand-, sphagnum-, or (multi-
ply-ascending according to topographical or geographical loca-

tion), cedar-, tamarack-, sago-, et cetera. I could make use of poetic license, grind in a little rhetoric, smudge on some petty lies, and sprinkle it all liberally with balderdash. And all the while your botanist-ecologist is assiduously measuring the salinity of water, testing the acidity of soils and, in a word, behaving in a scientific manner altogether exemplary and praiseworthy; being far too busy to tell you of bogs and swampy places. It is left to me. But rhetoric, poetry—even lies—all flooding forth in the splendid flow and rhythm that English can provide, cannot substitute for the scientists' learning, nor for even a simple appreciation of natural beauty.

Since I have already confessed to not knowing one whit about botanical nomenclature, how can I then explain about the differences between these ecological habitats? I cannot—as such, that is. Surely "swamp," "bog," and "marsh" are only synonymous terms for a muddy hole filled with water. It is true. But varying temperatures, elevations, soils, and water—and, in particular, the plants which grow in these varied situations, all make for a sound reasoning behind the many labels. In a word, though no botanist, I know these places, and have a great bond of sympathy for them. I will not endeavor laboriously to itemize aquatic plants, pondweeds, and grasses; but I can tell you that these plain, simply contrived lances of green are beautifully clean and in harmony with their surroundings. "Swamp" is merely a vague name—like "jungle"—not really meaning anything, but decidedly wet. To me it means southern cypress boles, white ibis and anhingas, Louisiana herons and Bachman's warbler; hot, humid nights, clematis, and Cherokee rose. "Bog" brings into focus the redolence of sweet-scented fragrances and springy mosses; the clarity of clear water running over white sands; the beauty of stunted conifers, bog plants, and orchids; the feel of sponginess and black stones, and memories of a scent and spirit everywhere. "Marsh" means mud and vivid greens and yellows in grasses; swaying Blue flag irises and warm sunlit days; the nesting of Marsh wrens; the sight and sound of gallinules and Red-winged blackbirds, of pungent odors and soft breezes. A "fen" is miles of marsh, crisscrossed by low dikes and small canals, filled with waterfowl and sedges; cool and windy; smelling of wet earth. A "morass" or a "quagmire" are any of these in which one becomes miserably stuck; and a "slough" is much the same, only add "despond" (this for my fellow admirers of Bunyan). A "water meadow" is filled with blue water, moor hens rising over the reeds, herons in stately progress between partly submerged tussocks, and a distant countryside all wrapped in the soft, comatose peace of a summer haze. The kinds of herbage and the loveliness inherent in such places can be learned neither from the sober ecologist (who will admit to computational exactitude) nor from me (who admits to an unbridled romanticism). You will get very wet learning about them, and tired, and inconceivably muddy; but you must learn yourself of the charms of swamps, marshes, and wet places. You will find it worthwhile.

I have told you that we have here a fresh and a salt marsh. Both and, even, adjacent. Each has its charm. But we have lost our bog. On the other end of our woods from that gully in which used to grow Yellow Lady's-slippers, further housing has advanced, as fire before a wind slowly isolates a copse, then creeps back and around to engulf it. A "southern colonial" house—so advertised by a sign—squats solidly in the middle of "my bog." The land surely enough belonged to someone else, and I cannot complain of them using it as they might wish, but "southern colonial"? All in green wood, peeling paint, and imitation stone. Oh yes, and it has a blue-mirrored globe set atop a concrete pedestal. All of this squats upon my bog, as I said . . . all perhaps sinking (as I did not say, wishing not to be uncharitable) but covering forever the green tussocks of marsh grass, the bright meadow flowers, and the last abode, here, of Meadow mice. Now Meadow mice are painfully common everywhere. But not here. Here they lived only in this small bog. Now the bog is gone and the Meadow mice with it. More such mice will come, but more such bogs will not. It is a small thing indeed, the loss of this bog. But it is in small things that loss is felt; it is by the disappearance of first one thing, then another, that—quite suddenly —we are alone.

I hadn't seen a Yellow-bellied sapsucker for years, and last week I saw two. They were hitching around and around a large old apple tree in the orchard, drilling their orderly rows of holes to get sap, and watching for the hapless insects which would become stuck in it. This handsome woodpecker is more often belabored than any other bird as the butt of dreadful plays on words revolving about its name. I once saw a fat man nearly inhale his cigar in laughter when a mild and bespectacled little teacher innocently said he'd seen one of these birds. But my annoyance turned to amusement when I heard the mild little man—maintaining a perfectly straight face—go on to describe in detail such species as the "Bellan Owl" and the "Abercrombian Finch." The fat man finally saw that he was being turned into the fool, and quickly left.

The Yellow-bellied sapsucker has a yellow belly: not a yellow chest, nor "underside," nor "ventral portion," nor "stomach"—

but "belly." And he sucks sap—not quite like sipping soda through a straw; but licking it, slurping it, or whatever, he slathers it down with relish and with it the insects he is seeking as well . . . (herein I pause for any fat men with cigars to burst into guffaws). It is, perhaps, of no interest to either cigar-smokers or to you, but the Yellow-bellied sapsucker nearly always sits on his tail (this, I promise you, is literally applied) at an angle of 45 degrees. The ends of his tail are fashioned into rather bristly sharp points, for sitting. If he has either a warped personality or a jaundiced eye, I know nothing of it. But his eggs are quite round and pure white. His mother's were, anyhow. (One cannot be too careful these days.)

I have not for nine years seen a Red-headed woodpecker; and I can think of no satisfactory reason why. They were once very commonly seen throughout the East. It is not that they are gone entirely, just diminished. But they are diminished to a fine point indeed. To my observation, they are simply no longer here, that is all. And it is a shame, for they are a gay and striking bird, boisterous and vibrant. Their black, white, and red plumage and their quick, flamboyant movements are enough to "give one's heart a change of mood"—to loosely paraphrase Robert Frost —and to brighten any woodland corner. My last bird flew to the telephone pole across from the barn and orchard, trilled a guttural tattoo, and then drummed a long roll in quick response. He sat for a moment, flipped over in a wide arc as might a flycatcher, returned, and exuberantly drummed again. He looked down at me boldly and unafraid as I sat on a log to watch him. How his head shone in the sun, and how starkly his white patches gleamed against the blue-black of his dark feathers! He cocked his head once again, hitched half round the pole, and flew off over the small McIntosh, to the left of the Rome Beauties and in between the Delicious and a Seckel pear. Nine years later I can still trace the path of his trajectory in my mind, and can yet see him flying out of my life and into the golden brightness of that morning.

June

"What Is So Rare..."

June is often petulant during her infancy—even cool—but by her teens she straightens away into a warm creature with an airy grace, and in maturity has the stability and beauty of dignified age. June has a strength of mint-freshness that the middle-age of August cannot match. June leaves are newly coined and sharp, with little dust, jagged insect holes, or faded hues. Her grass is tall and straight, her flowers firm and unbent. That is her usual pattern. This June, however, flew in from the gate of May like a fiery hussy, shook off her shawl in a sharp summer storm in which she smashed her beads against the lawn and rent the garden with her breath; then she lay quietly and clutched us to her flaming bosom. Everything wilted. A week passed, and still there was only a quiet and oppressive heat. Not before the seventh did a cool breeze come out of the northwest to break the spell.

On the morning of the eighth of June, as did everyone else, I felt a surge of freedom. I dropped my work where it lay; gathered up some pots, flower flats, and a shovel; called my old dog, and drove south. I didn't mean to go far. It was only that not long before I had been telling you of bogs, and I felt an urge to muck about in one. Besides, a particular orchid (according to a map drawn for me on an old envelope a long time ago by David Fables) was to be found in bloom on this date, and I had always wanted to photograph it in color. The place designated was in the dead heart of the Jersey Pine Barrens, 50 miles away. We drove southward: dog's head out the window, and mine somewhat dreamily in the clouds.

We (dog and me) first began to see the barrens' Pitch pines only 15 miles from home. There were rolling sand hills just below the level of Asbury Park. I saw a crushed Red squirrel on the road and, further on, an equally defunct Barred owl. The road began to straighten out, and soon there were only low pines on either side. I passed Lakewood, turned left, and drove southeast. Here there were only the stunted pines and white sand, the black bitumen road cutting a straight ribbon through the seemingly sterile landscape.

Within barely an hour I had reached the spot; an obscure, flat stream denoted only by a small metal culvert fence and a few feet of white railing. There was nothing in either direction for miles, neither houses nor cars. I parked the car, and the dog, in just three bounces, found herself belly-deep in black mud. I pulled her out by her collar, her long legs, now ebony, looking ridiculous against her white and fawn body. I saw with my binoculars that orchids did seem to be blooming on the far edge of the bog, so I collected my equipment and, dog at heel, waded into the mire.

I had been told when I received permission to enter the bog there was no quicksand—but you are always even more careful, I think, when warned there is *not* something. There was not, at any rate. I found it a safe bog and kind. It grew to be very hot, but that was nothing I blamed on the bog. There were some acres of very substantial mud flats into which one sank not at all. Then, of a sudden, there would be a soft area and we would sink to my knees and the dog's belly. We would pull each other out and go ahead slowly. There were islands in the mud of sphagnum and grasses on which dwarfed White cedar and pitcher plants were in abundance. Hundreds of sundews—another carnivorous bog plant—were everywhere, their tiny, curling tentacles as sticky as the "flypaper" they actually were. There was Sheep laurel in bloom and other flowers with which I was unfamiliar. I found yet another, taller sundew, which also was in bloom: a single violet-hued flower on a stalk bearing other unopened buds, all in a row. The whole plant was only 6 inches high. This was *Drosera filiformis;* the Round-leaved sundew is *Drosera rotundifolia.* Further on, I found a deeper pool in which the Bladderwort seemed to thrive. The species of pitcher plant was *Sarracenia purpurea;* it, too, was in bloom and had a tall, almost waxlike dark red or light green flower. The curious fly-catching pitchers were narrow at the bases, bulbous in the centers, and opened up into an upright cup. The cup was half-filled with a sticky liquid and tiny, fine hairs grew downward to prevent the ascent of any small insect luckless enough to fall into the cup. The insects were devoured—having fallen into the wicked syrup—by the unspectacular method of being turned into a gruel and digested; very unlike the Venus's flytrap with its imaginative springs and jaws.

Finally, there were my orchids. The one which I was so earnestly seeking was in full bloom and I gave sincere thanks to the shade of Dave Fables. This was the beautiful *Arethusa bulbosa,* a rich magenta orchid, delicately scented and only 8 or 9 inches high. The single flower was only an inch and a half in height, semi-erect, with magenta petals and a bearded lip containing three white ridges spotted with magenta. The stalk was pale green and there were no leaves—only a single solitary leaf appears after the flowering season. The "root" is only a small corm, smaller than a crocus bulb. I took a dozen close photographs in color from all angles and every point of vantage. I also took one of the dog, who, in miscalculating a leap over a pool, had unceremoniously landed in a spatter of mud, and was magically changed from a greyhound into a spotted Dalmatian. She looked chagrined, and her picture showed it. The *Arethusa* pictures were superb and will be a constant reminder of that sparkling day. There were other orchids to be seen, but they were not yet in bloom. One was the Grass Pink, *Colopogon pulchellus*, and the enchantingly fragile-looking (though not actually fragile) *Pogonia ophioglossoides*, the not badly named "Snake-mouth orchid," for its flower's drooping lip does somewhat resemble a snake's jaws agape.

We pottered round in the mud for hours, both dog and man completely content. I gathered specimens of sundews and pitcher plants and, with the sanction of the owner, dug up a Sheep laurel. But I did not touch the orchids, such being sacrosanct. I walked or slogged my way over to the meandering stream, itself not a part of the bog pools, and was surprised to find it cool and clear, running only inches deep, over pure white sand. The bog mud and sphagnum just stopped, it seemed, and there was firm white sand. The water, though clear, was stained the color of light tea; I took it to be colored by the cedar roots over which it ran. Dog and man were soon washed clean of mud; the cool water felt refreshing and the sand was smooth, not granular, between the toes. In a mood of mutual well-being, we slowly walked up the shallow stream to the road and found the car. The scents of evening were just beginning to rise when we drove off, and I heard the whine of but a single mosquito.

One word more, perhaps, about orchids. According to books, orchids are "perennial herbs having ingenious devices to insure the plant of pollination; having three sepals colored like petals, and two lateral petals, below which is a 'lip' conspicuously colored, often spurred, and containing nectar for the attraction of insects." All of this is related with no tongue in cheek—and no mention of any nectar "for the attraction of humans." For orchids are not only expensive and another bauble of the well-to-do, they are perhaps the most beautiful flower in the world. They are exquisite, delicate yet hardy, soft-hued, and lovely; and come in every imaginable shape and size. They are either white, green, purple, brown, yellow, magenta, or even red. Most are of pastel shades and are principally tropical, though many are hardy denizens of the far north and of quite high elevations.

Some have roots, some corms, and some are "air plants" having no roots at all.

Orchids have many commercial uses, but the most well-known is the production of vanilla extract, a direct derivation of the pods of *Vanilla planifolia*, a large tropical orchid. It is interesting to note in passing that the Aztec name for their orchid was "tlilxochitl"—quite a mouthful for "I'll take vanilla." In New Guinea I found veritable "forests" of hanging orchids in the humid rain forests of the coast and orchids of all kinds in the very cool moss forests of the highest elevations. I have seen them in Panama, in Bermuda, in Tahiti, and in scores of tropical towns all blooming vigorously and lending a breathless beauty to even the most sordid of hovels. In New Guinea the men (not the women) wear them in their hair.

Native orchids—that is, native to the United States—are scarcely less charming, but hardly in any way equalling the magnificence of many tropical varieties. Many of ours are confined to bogs, or at least to an acid soil. Among our most spectacular are the *Cypripedieae*, the "slipper" orchids or Moccasin flowers. Perhaps our most regal one is *C. reginae*, the Queen Lady's-slipper. I have seen it only rarely in New Jersey, and then only in Sussex County, the most mountainous and northwesterly of our counties. *C. pubesceous* is the yellow and is more commonly found; I have seen it in a dozen places. *C. acaule* is the pink; quite common, as I have mentioned. These are all we have of slipper orchids in New Jersey, although others are to be found in the West. These plants are most interesting in their mechanical adaptation for pollination. The slipper is not precisely that, for the name "orchid" itself is derived from the Greek word for "testicle"—although it indeed, also, resembles the puckered toe of a moccasin. At any rate, it is an elongated pouch with a small opening at the top end near the stem. Over the opening is a sort of trap door which, though allowing access to bees and other pollinating insects, forces them to brush it with their backs as they leave with their burdens of pollen.

Our moccasin orchids also produce a volatile oil which, rendered into a drug called "Fluid extract of Cypripedium, U.S.P.," is used as a diaphoretic, nerve stimulant, and antispasmodic in the treatment of hysteria, neuralgia, chorea, hypochondria, and, to a degree, epilepsy.

The only orchid of the genus *Orchis* is the lovely Showy Orchis, *Orchis spectabilis*. It grows in hardwood forests in many places in New Jersey, but I have never seen it here. It has mauve and white flowers, a half-dozen or so to a stalk, each about an inch long. The leaves themselves are broad and showy.

The very lovely Bearded orchid, the Grass Pink, and the Arethusa I have mentioned; these, and the Rattlesnake plantains. Among others are the *Spiranthes*, tall, small-flower orchids with oddly twisted stems; one, at least, of these "Ladies'-tresses" is found here. And yet others are the *Habenarias*—so named because they have a "strap" or loose rein left hanging below the flower. These are our "fringe" orchids, and are beautiful indeed for they are tall plants with many flowers in a cluster at the top of a long stem. I have found only the white here at home, but both yellow, purple, and orange species are known. These are only our best known; there are still many others.

Perhaps I have run on too long talking of orchids—but I find them a never-ending source of enjoyment, not only for their beauty but for the enjoyment i find in searching them out amidst bogs, rich woodlands, and cool damp ravines. Native orchids, with some of the ferns, I find among the most satisfying of all flowers.

In June of every year there appears out of nowhere what we have come to call "Barbara's Bane." This dreadful occurrence is the influx of helpless nestlings that are foisted off upon us by local amateur zoo keepers. Carried home in cupped hands by thousands of children each early summer are countless hapless and forlorn creatures plucked either from the nest or made off with just at the one moment of real vulnerability in their lives, their "schooling." This heterogenous admixture comes to us at all hours of the night or day: baby squirrels, rabbits, raccoons, bats, thrushes, sparrows, mice, snakes, turtles, and more than one "pet bug"—one of these being, once, a caterpillar-hunter beetle of a metallic green, quite a pretty thing, really. Some are not babies at all, but downright mean and exasperated adults who take a dim view indeed of all that pawing about. Others are scarcely out of the egg, blind, naked, and wet. Yet others are sick. Sick or not, most are poorly handled at one time or another and surely die. It is irritating to see some proper lady permit the keeping of a young animal, letting it be mauled by her children, starved or overfed, pulled at, pummelled, and worn to tatters; and then, when the poor creature is about to breathe its last (and no doubt looking forward to a mercifully quick end), this lady will tra-la her way to our door, twittering like a fool, and then be off in a shot to spare herself the end she surely knows will come. And there we are, left to watch it die. And, generally, it does. But not infrequently there is the lingering departure, our earnest ministrations for long days and longer nights, some rays of hope—and then the unfortunate thing dies anyway. It is a dreary task.

But sometimes there is a shining light of success. In fact, we have had not a few startling recoveries. A wild duck, covered with oil from a leaking tanker, was cleaned, fed, cured, and released. A loon in the same predicament was treated and freed. A dozen or two songbirds or more survived and became quite tame. The day we found an albino wild rabbit was the prelude to a long visit—and he was a wild albino, no nonsense about that. Many wild things did get well and go "merrily off into the greenwood" (there, probably, to meet a quick end because of their tameness). We did not try to "tame" anything, actually, hoping to keep them as wild as possible—but some things were simply by nature as tame as could be. Once we had a herring gull with a crippled wing and once a totally blind chipmunk.

I have, in the past (now I have better sense), kept falcons. I once had eight birds in the shed I called my "mews," and was nearly driven to distraction in efforts to feed them all on fresh

mice or liver and bone meal. I was the worst falconer imaginable
—but I "looked good," at least to the uninitiated. Surely enough
I raised each, eyas or haggard, to a point just a scant breath away
from a kill (this to my credit)—but some dread thing always
happened: a broken wing, damaged feathers that were beyond
"imping," illness or disease. One bright day my best bird simply
fell off his hoop (this was a short-winged hawk) and broke his
wing. Just like that. All that beauty and fire and spirit gone in
an instant. The mended wing became infected and I had to kill
him.

It was no little pleasure to have hawks. I "walked them" for
hours each day, they sitting straight and regal on my gloved fist.
I got to know them well in training and to love them. Their cruel
beaks and talons held no terror for me, and their brilliant yellow
eyes no deceit. My hawks were strong and good. Only one
ever bolted for freedom, and he was new and untrained. All of
the rest would mount high and dash downward in tremendous
stoops to the swinging lure, or (the Accipiters) come smashing
through the trees to pounce and scream. None of them ever got
to kill a sparrow, however.

After a time, losing first one, then another, I grew to be saddened somewhat by their loyalty. They would stare for long
minutes at feral hawks, craning their necks when the wild birds
flew out of sight. Before long I set them all free—those few that
were left. I have never kept another, and probably never shall
again. Somehow I have grown to feel that to be wild and free
is the most important thing of all for animals.

One wild thing was anything but unhappy in our company.
Some years ago, along with a porridge of other wild things, Barbara was brought a young mockingbird. She fed and cared for
it, and it became quite tame. Then there came the day for setting
him loose. Only he would not leave. When we retreated into
the house he haunted the windows until he found an opening,
and then back he was, flying all over the house as though he
owned it. He stayed and stayed, coming and going as he pleased.
I remember one particular day in late summer when Barbara, for

some occasion or other, had over twenty ladies all stacked up on the lawn drinking tea and crooning about gardening, I believe it was. One of them looked up to call attention to the mockingbird, which had flown into a high tree nearby. Barbara said, "Oh yes, he's mine"—at which point she whistled and down flew the bird to alight on her shoulder. Then he sat on her head, had a morsel of cake, and left, leaving the ladies' mouths ajar.

Of all wild creatures, the hardest to raise seem to be young rabbits. Even with the most tender care, sterilized nipples, regular fifteen-minute feeding even through the night, and exactly measured amounts of food, they still often die. Last year, however, after someone had left a grass-lined basket at our door, we somehow achieved success and had the pleasure of releasing all four of the babes as three-quarter-grown rabbits, and of watching them for many weeks, as they seldom strayed beyond the confines of the yard.

The calloused will say of this, "Why bother?" You know full well, however, why we bother. It is because we have little choice. I might indeed "put them to sleep," which is the cowardly way of saying "knock them on the head." Actually, knocking them firmly on the head is the best way—often more humane, by far, than injection badly done (which it often is). But that is all another matter. We shall go on with this "animal hospice" sort of thing—feeding, curing, burying—and hope for the best. There is no other way. "Barbara's Bane" is the bane of us all, the price of human compassion. It is a quality other animals do not possess. And it is often for this reason alone that I am led to believe that mankind may yet survive.

Seeing young birds seldom fails to remind me of the "Screech Owl School." Never mind how much it resembles the infantile appellations of certain nursery schools—this one is truly just what it says: a school *for* Screech owls *by* Screech owls.

You must first be assured that I am not saying this in jest. I am not. Young birds must be taught much by their parents; basic instincts only go part of the way. But although I had seen instances before of somewhat similar behavior patterns, I had never been fortunate enough to witness anything like this.

We were all quietly sitting on the back porch one calm, warm June night. We had dined outside for no other reason than that it had seemed a good idea. The smoke remained of a charcoal fire, and there was wax blown on things by too energetic a blowing out of candles. Barbara was engaged at that moment in showing the youngest how to blow and how not to blow. "Now blow," she said, in the time-honored phrase of all mothers.

After the blowing session we all simply sat. It had been a splendid meal and I, for one, was replete. It was the pleasantest thing to do—just sit and quietly absorb the descent of night. And as we all sat there we heard a Screech owl's cry, so close that we could not help being startled.

Our attention now zeroed-in on Screech owls, we saw that there seemed to be an owl on the stubs of some branches I had cut from a tall tulip poplar, some 40 feet away. Yes, we all agreed, there certainly was an owl. And below that another, and yet another, and another below the last; five in all. It seemed obvious that the highest one was the parent bird. She was busy and officious, puffing out like a balloon or slicking down as slim as a rod—these contortions evidently influenced by whatever she was saying. And she was certainly volubly saying something: her throat feathers worked furiously, and she emitted a continual series of guttural sounds or croaks and mutterings to those below —undoubtedly her brood. The brood acted just as stupid and simple-minded as any children act when they are all lined up and being taught something. They just sat like morons and stared down their noses.

The mother (for we all agreed it was certainly she) began working up and down, and flapped her wings. She increased the volume of her mutterings and repeated the same thing. Then she vaulted from the perch and plummeted downward, striking the ground. She looked back over her shoulder, then flew back to her perch. She repeated this procedure twice. Then she hopped to a stub occupied by a young owl. She nudged it. It continued to sit and stare stupidly.

Suddenly she gave another "proper" Screech-owl cry, left the perch, and flew into the woods in an instant, leaving the young owls sitting there.

We carefully noted that the young owls then came to life. Two of them started hopping and working their wings after the fashion of their mother. The third watched them with interest, while the last still sat in a pet. It seemed to us that the brightest and largest were at the top of the row of perches (possibly females, which are normally larger), and that the less bright were further down the ladder—but all of this may have been pure accident, if, in fact, the case.

Within minutes two adult owls reappeared, each with a mouse. The less bustling one, which we took for the male, sat on a high limb with his mouse. He didn't eat it. He simply held it. Meanwhile, the "mother" (our opinion) flew to the same perch she had previously stood on, and transferred the mouse from her beak to her claws. Then she made a considerable lot of talk, all low. She then flew down from her perch to the ground with the mouse (again in her beak), and returned immediately without the mouse. More talk. Then she bolted off and pounced down onto the dead mouse, to return with it to a low perch. Twice again she repeated carrying the mouse down, leaving, and again dropping on it in attack.

The young owls, now aroused by the sight of the mouse, were all leaning forward on their separate branch stubs. Finally, one leaned too far and awkwardly parachuted down in the direction of the mouse, which the mother had left on the ground. The young one *walked* to the mouse in a series of flopping hops —and this unowlish display brought the mother down in a flash. She grabbed the mouse in her beak and pushed it into the youngster's mouth, and then she "herded" him over the grass until he finally flew weakly to the lowest branch stub, and, in doing so, dropped the mouse. The mother retrieved it and went to another branch.

Meanwhile, the darkening of the night just about obliterated any more reliable recordings of action: after that we "thought" we saw things. As our eyes watered from staring into the dusky woods, our last genuine record of this event was the sight of the young owls going up and down the branches as though they were on a tall ladder; and the sight, also, of the least aggressive of the youngsters finally trying his turn and falling flat on his face!

We never learned what the male did with his mouse. But the schooling went on long after the curtain was rung down on us. Later we tried to use a flashlight to see their progress, but only succeeded in putting an end to the whole thing, for the "school" soon melted away into the woods.

The next night we waited anxiously for the school to start again, but no owls came. We did hear them in the woods, however, much later in the evening—and it seemed (though, of course, we can never be certain) that they were doing much the same thing. For some number of nights we heard rather more of the Screech owls than usual, and then they seemed to fade back into the gray-green tapestry of trees as normalcy again reigned.

The smallest boy came bursting in, slamming the screen door, not too long ago, with a dead sunfish he'd "caught." Well, he *had* caught it—it just happened it was dead when he caught it—a mere matter of circumstance. He called it a "sunny." And a sunny it was; I had called it the same thing when I was a boy. It was indeed a sunfish. "Everybody knows a sunfish," I related to my little girl, who had come rushing in to "see the sunny." "A sunfish is like a bass," I said in a tone of authority.

"But what is a bass like?" she asked.

I considered this question for a long moment before I answered. Although I had caught many bass in my lifetime, and had eaten as many more, and would have considered that I "knew bass"—I also knew that being wrong in a hypothesis is one thing, but that random "guessing" is a breach of adult responsibility when answering a child. Thus, not only had the sunfish been caught, so had I. I said, "I don't know." And down came the reference books.

Sunfish, we all discovered together, are a family among the

"Perch-like fishes" of the Order *Perciformes.* That, perhaps, was no news. We read on to find that bass (or, more properly, basses) are under a separate family, the *Serranidae.* But both the Small-mouth and the Large-mouth "basses" are actually sun-fishes. "Ah ha," cried the children. And so we read further to see that fishes are not separated by dentition and characteristics of cranial form, as are mammals, but by a counting and meas-uring of fins, spines, scales, and, seemingly quite important, the location of a "lateral line." (We found this on our fish, and it was just that.) We also found there were many other considera-tions, such as whether or not there were "teeth on the tongue" (ours had no teeth). The children all learned how to spell "ichthyologist," as well.

It seems that the Small-mouth "bass" is of a genus called *Micropterus,* and their dorsal (top) fin is separated by a deep notch. The true sunfish—genus *Leponis*—have ten dorsal spines and a notched tail. Crappies—genus *Pomoxis*—have long heads and concave foreheads. And there you are. *Exeunt* sunfishes.

Can we just pop the lid on them and forget them? Indeed you may. And I agree with you that, having been forced to review this annotation of dry genera, who might be expected to enquire further? Who could care if a half-bucket of the smelly, wet things—all sharp spikes and slime—might or might not have "a prominent spot on the gill cover," eleven anal fin rays, or "a brassy belly."

"Brassy bellies" or not—these fresh-water fishes in our pond all have their proper names and their proper places. Some, like the Small-mouth bass and sunfishes are carnivorous and prevent the pond from becoming overcrowded. Others, the small shiners, dace, Killifishes, chubs, and sticklebacks, feed on the larvae of many insects and, as well, provide food for the larger fishes. And the catfishes and suckers are bottom feeders which provide useful service in keeping the water clean. Since no pickerel are in our pond, the king is certainly the Small-mouth bass. It is one of the most acclaimed by anglers, as has been said by Henshall: "he has the arrowy rush and vigor of a trout, the untiring strength and bold leap of a salmon, while he has a system of fighting tactics peculiarly his own. I consider him, inch for inch and pound for pound, the gamest fish that swims." The children cast by the hour for these strong-willed fish, and one way or another—sometimes, even, being reduced to worms—somehow seem to get their share. I well remember a particular incident: I came upon the two older boys fishing in the late evening at the side of the pond. Two grown men were rigged like wireless stations with every imaginable kind of fish line and fish lure, having fun for themselves. The tale is so old, it cries out for oblivion; of course, the boys got the bass, the fishermen got nothing, I was quietly proud, the fish was large and sizzled in the pan. The tale *is* old. But it will be told again. And fishermen will listen; they have, for a long time . . .

> *E'en in sleep I'm bound*
> *To dream of fishing, as of crusts the hound—*
>   THEOCRITUS, IDYLL XXI

But what of trout in these woods? None, you say? Not a bit of it—this sounds like sheer bravado, I know. But I will explain.

Of course we have no native trout left, any more than native moose. But the Fireman's Pond, over in that group of houses of which I have often spoken (here in New Jersey the term "village" is used only by way of affectation—but that is what it is, more-or-less), has fine, fresh, clear water in it, and is liberally stocked with trout. These trout are of the usual kind hatcheries put out: Rainbows, Browns, and Brook trout. No doubt about this fish being of a noble sort—even hatchery-bred and dumped from a large can into a lazy pond half-filled with pickerel weed. The trout is a regal fish. My father used to take me, as a boy, to the Old West Brook, in then-wild Passaic County, where I saw him deftly cast his fly and fill his creel. How well I remember the sweet grass that lined the creel and the trout lying in iridescent splendor, all shimmering in gold and silver; the pleasant fishy odor; and my father's shining face. He is old now, but still he fills his creel, and in the Old West Brook. I have since cast flies of my own, in waters famous for trout—in Colorado and Alaska. And in New Zealand I saw trout that were large enough to make a fisherman tremble and pale. But I am shockingly poor at this casting compared to those who are truly adept at the sport. Fireman's Pond trout may be nursery-bred, but a trout is a good fish—and a good dish.

My saying that trout are in our woods is true. A certain number of them are swept over the weir at the lower end of the pond, and the stream that issues forth from this small waterfall empties into an arm of the estuary; that is, into salt water. The water, then, in this long cove is brackish, but trout can and do survive in it and apparently even venture further out into truly salt water, for they are on the Marine Laboratory list of fishes found in the waters around Sandy Hook. But our woods come into it because the trout do, evidently, try to find again the swift streams which it is in their nature to seek. There is another, lower, weir

on our side of the long cove, and trout do jump over it and into the shallow pond above. Then, most likely because it is so shallow, and therefore warm, they continue up the very tiny rivulet which feeds that pond. This slender stream is curiously narrow —only a foot or two wide in most places—but it is spring-fed, cold, and moves at a fair pace. Thus do we have trout in our woods. We never fish for them, preferring to go from time to time just to watch them dart away, just for the joy of knowing that they are trout and in our woods. Of course, some enterprising boy does, once in a great while, discover their identity and fish them out. But more have always come.

There is a lovely, old, stone church at the nearby crossroads. It has a charming hillside aspect, windows of stained glass, and a great bronze bell by whose deep and sonorous clangor the faithful are called. Each year during the last week in June a charity fair is held. There are stalls behind the church in which pies and cakes are sold. Also sold are plants and herbs, rummage and antiques, old books, and suitable refreshments. There is a small carousel for the children, and games, pony riding, and the like. Music of a kind is piped through a box, and people come from miles around. Not that the same thing is not happening in a thousand parishes throughout the land, but one's own, it always seems, is far and away the best. The Stone Church Fair is to summer what the Race Meet is to the fall.

Also a summery thing is the annual Strawberry Festival at the local firehouse. "All you can eat" reads the sign. Here again there is loud music, lights strung in garish splendor, and the two gleaming engines all sparkling red and striped with gold. All their brass is shining like mirrors, and on the doors of one engine are painted the stern, aquiline features of a Navesink Indian. I think I shall never forget the time I first met the man who has since been my attorney for over a dozen years. The firehouse was gay with colored lights, and the road had been cordoned off for dancing. Square dancing there was in plenty, but at the height of the gaiety some youngsters became impatient for the current dance rage, which, at that time, was the "Bunny Hop." All in the spirit of ripe strawberries and highly volatile punch, I was induced to join in—and my first meeting with my now good friend took place as we were both "Bunny Hopping" down the road in tow of our wives, trying to say "How do you do," but actually saying "How do you do-do-do . . ." as we hop-hop hopped.

July

Of Wasps and Sundials

The loudest noise I can ever remember hearing is the boom of the great brass cannon that is annually detonated here on the evening of the Fourth of July. There are firecrackers on every hand, flags, children running about with sparklers, and an enormous lawn on which people mill around seeking points of vantage for their collapsible wooden chairs. The heavy cannon is laboriously hauled to the forefront by an orderly squad of men dressed in Continental Army uniforms. The piece is loaded with powder, rammed, and secured. There is a standing-to-attention, a rolling of drums, and the lanyard is pulled. The noise is an overwhelming blast—so loud, as I say, that hands are clapped to ears, children cry, and men can feel the deep concussion in every fiber of their bodies. After this there is the main fireworks display, which inevitably terminates with the American flag done up in exploding lights, shrieking fireballs, violent explosions, and, rising into the velvet sky, a halo of smoke cascading light and fury. Then everyone sorts out the children, who are still spilling lemonade and sitting in it; there is the clacking of folding chairs being folded; there is the ubiquitous comment on how bright the stars are now that it's over; and everyone goes home.

July is thus launched. And then the heat begins. Not that it is always hot, or that any sirocco burns off the desert to scorch us . . . but July is hot, no getting round the fact. Sometimes there are thunder showers and the steaming earth seems to turn itself into a vapor that is pleasant but, oh, so hot. The children are scarcely ever seen, being each day immersed in salt water the day long. Usually, even the showers are scarce and everything turns dry; the grass, shrubs, and even the oak woods take on a fine glaze of dust. The chickens wallow in a comatose stupor in their dust baths, the ducks stay in their little pool, and I, under the cool shade of the great tulip poplars that rise behind the barn, fling open the loft doors and coax in what there may be of an occasional sea breeze.

Under this tremendous blanket of heat it is true that most wild things take cover. Rabbit and fox lie each under his own tree root or grass bank until the fall of darkness and something like a coolness rises from the baking ground. Birds are under the thickest and most impenetrable of foliage. Only the vireos make any attempt to sing, or a crow might caw lazily, as though disturbed from his dream.

But there is one tribe of *Animalia* that thrives, and even flourishes, in the dry heat of July. These are the insects. Ants are scurrying everywhere, their tunnel entrances piled high into cones of fine sand. The dung beetle rolls his ball in the same patient way he did in June. Water striders and damsel flies haunt the pond and stream, leaf hoppers and aphids plague the garden, and butterflies visit every flower and lend color to the arid beds. But the most joyous of all among this large family are the wasps and bees. My barn is filled with their comings and goings, and bees are everywhere on flower heads in a delirium of pollen gathering. One bumblebee I saw today had not only his leg sacs overloaded, but his face as well was filled with the yellow pollen, as though he'd been struck with a custard pie . . . and a wasp had captured a spider so large that she had to drag it behind her like a sack of meal.

In the sparsely grassed, leaf-littered bank in front of the house, just at the wood's edge, there lives a particular kind of wasp. I came to notice her not because she made herself obtrusive, but because I had reread, after long years, a particular book. I had taken down a dusty box of books from "grandpa's attic," got it home, left it on the edge of the rug, and tripped over it for a full day, before (after kicking it) I finally sat down to open it. The first book out was something very like *The Wireless Boys' Trip to Nicaragua*. The second was the book of which I speak.

It was a worn volume by Fabre, the gentle old French scientist who spent his life studying insects. I felt again that childlike awe that had prompted my first battered but cherished butterfly collection. The next day I proceeded to ferret out the entire set of *Souvenirs Entomologiques* and carefully began to read them all. I learned of gray worms and beetles and cruel mantises, but most of all I found my imagination taken by wasps. I had thought I knew a great deal about wasps. I found I knew next to nothing, as I read of the lives of these remarkable specialists. I learned that among the solitary wasps were those that pursued but one species of one genus of beetle; that this beetle, because of its hardened armor plate and capabilities for defense, must be attacked with a precision more adept than any fencing master's —an agility more supple than a ballerina's. This wasp must function by feinting and dodging and passing through the defense of her antagonist and, in all the fury and turmoil of that struggle, must pierce the one small unprotected spot between all that armor; and, once having found this, must penetrate most deftly with her poison stinger to pierce the one of many nerve ganglia that will render him helpless. Once, by some miracle of precision, that is accomplished, and the great beetle lies paralyzed, she must then drag his inert form some hundred feet, or yards perhaps, to the earthen chamber which she had previously dug to conform to his exact size.

Such stories went on, each more bizarre and fascinating than the last. One, with which I found myself enthralled, concerned a kind of wasp which, after preying upon her single historic foe, finds that she herself becomes prey to a parasitic fly scarcely as large as her head. The fly is even more swift than she, and its target is not her body, but, more subtly, her future young. It waits, with infinite patience, near the entrance of her underground retreat, to which she must go with her own vanquished prey. The fly springs into action, not at her appearance in the distance, nor even when she arrives close by, heavily laden, orienting her position. It times its headlong rush to that exact moment when, as the wasp reaches her covered entranceway, she must for an instant lay aside her victim to lift the obstruction she had left there as protection. At that precise moment the wily fly dashes to the body of the wasp's victim, lays an egg, and is gone in a flicker out of harm's way. The wasp, if she fails to see this action, goes on with her business of storing her victim, and lays her own egg that her young may later feed upon him. The result is that the fly's egg, upon hatching, is larger than the wasp's; the fly larva then consumes not only its weaker rival but the fresh meal so carefully prepared for it as well.

To end that particular story on a more hopeful note—for it would appear we had left the wasp to a hopeless end—it seems that, often, the wasp wins the race with the fly and prevents her egg being laid. Many other tales, all true and well documented, are told by Fabre of similar intrigues, plans thwarted, hairbreadth escapes, and justice or injustice applied.

I read all this, as I say, with awe. These wasps, however, and the sun-drenched acres which Fabre loved, were foreign to us. That was France about which Fabre spoke; his wasps were French wasps. But might not some of these be found also in our own woods? A thorough search through some numbers of modern volumes quickly showed me that many of the same families of wasps were indeed to be found here; but instead of a living and exciting exposure of equally wonderful details, I found only a parroting of arid facts. Yet other books, painfully sought out, yielded little better. I found now, as I had found in childhood, that there is no one but Fabre. Other authors, also expert in the

field, have tried to imitate him, but in no way can they approach the greatness of that very splendid and very wonderful old man.

My next recourse was to go through my door and into the yard with a simple glass jar. It is well we are alone in our woods, for my first attempts at catching wasps would have been most embarrassing to have had witnessed. I ran and I slipped. I stalked and I pounced. I fell into holes and cursed most nobly at slippery leaves and the rasps of holly. But I caught wasps.

I found that Fabre's old and dear friends were everywhere waiting. There was the long-waisted, delicate *Ammophila;* the hairy *Scolia;* the spider-hunting *Pompilus;* the white-booted *Trypoxylon; Eumenes,* the little potter wasp who builds tiny "Grecian" jugs; *Bembex,* the fly-eating, sturdy, sand dweller who "thumped" Fabre's umbrella; *Sphex,* his old favorite; the Cicada-killing *Sphecius,* a whole regiment of assorted paper wasps and hornets—and I came at last to know my old friend who yearly comes to my grass bank, a friend more welcome than the spring warblers or great flights of geese, *Cerceris. Cer-*

ceris, neatly arrayed in black with lemon-yellow bands; *Cerceris,* the weevil-hunter.

Within a short while I had found thirty-four kinds of wasps all within sight of the barn. I became aware, also, of bees: Leaf-cutting bees, Mason bees, bumblebees, and Mining bees. And bees led to flies. I was staggered: there were Crane flies, March flies, Tangle-veined flies, Snipe flies, Soldier flies, Dance flies, Robber, Spear-winged, Hump-backed, and Syrphid flies; Flesh flies, Botflies, Gallflies, Gadflies, Nimble flies, Big-eyed flies and even (though I refused to believe it at first) Flat-footed flies. But I always returned to my wasps.

In following Jean Henri Fabre as a loyal disciple, I have spent many happy hours searching for new wasps. That is, wasps that were new to me. Slowly my list mounted and I made quite a project of watching them in the area just outside the barn, and inside as well.

My barn study, for a few weeks in both the spring and fall, becomes rather an uncomfortable abode. It is at these times that *Polistes,* the paper wasp, is either feverishly getting herself set-tled for winter or feverishly getting herself unsettled to begin a new summer season. Her temper grows short at these times, and so does mine. There is an occasional clash between us, but gen-erally we only grumble rather than lock horns. Once she gets shaken down and into business in the spring, she is a good enough companion. Then, busy making paper, catching prey for her future progeny, and tending properly to her business, she hasn't the time to make a nuisance of herself.

Polistes is a colonial wasp, living cooperatively with her kind; other wasps are quite solitary and are known as such. One of these is my favorite, *Monobia,* the large black wasp so boldly banded in white. She lives in the ½-inch-diameter holes in the barn drilled by Carpenter bees, and her prey consists only of caterpillars—she flies in, heavily burdened, looking like a tor-pedo plane coming to attack.

Another is the fragile-looking *Ammophila,* whose body seems

almost to be separated by a pipeline. Her abdomen trails far
behind, but she is lightly built and infinitely graceful. Her prey
too is caterpillars, which she paralyzes with the skill of a surgeon.

Some of the wasps are only ¼-inch long, and others quite
gigantic. Some are oddly shaped, such as the *Pelecinid* wasp,
whose abdomen is five-sixths its total length; the tiny Chalcids,
which have a curious enlargement on their hind legs; the Horn-
tails, large and bulky; the Ichneumon wasps, which often have
tremendously large drills on their abdomens; and the bright emerald Cuckoo wasps which craftily lay their eggs with those of
another species. Nearly all use a barbless "hypodermic needle"
sheathed in their abdomens. (Only the bees have a barbed
stinger). Each has a certain amount of venom capable of killing
or paralyzing, but it is a tool, not a weapon. Fabre studied the
comparative effects and doses of wasp venom by submitting to
self-experiments involving the different species with which he
was familiar. It took me rather a long time before my interest
had gathered enough momentum to make me quite that curious.
But finally I arrived at that point. I allowed myself (most carefully) to be stung on the arm by certain species Fabre had
described. Of course, I expected he would be correct—I knew he
would be correct—but the cold-blooded business of being a
guinea pig had little appeal. What I found, however, could not
help but make my own experiment (which was not at all scientific, but mere curiosity) of great personal satisfaction. As did
Fabre, I found myself marvelling at the fact that *Sphex*—a large,
spectacular wasp—had the mildest sort of sting, with no reaction
whatever. *Ammophila*, too, was a mere nip. These are species
which most deftly stab their prey in a specific spot in their nerve
ganglia. Other wasps, such as the paper-making *Polistes*, whose
sting is less artful, have a sting of more healthy proportions. The
hornets (generally those wasps whose abdomens are more closely
connected with their thorax) are rather random and artless: *their*
sting is worth remembering and well worthy of a vow to stop
all such foolishness—which I promptly did, my arm swelling up
into the bargain. I never reached the point of testing the enor-

mous *Sphecius speciosus*, the so-called (and accurately called)
Cicada-killer, for the brute is an inch and a half long and seemingly the size of a hawk. Fabre insists, however, that even its sting
is not of dreadful consequence.

And one wasp more I gave a wide berth. It is a European import, a hornet, and its name is *Vespa crabro.* Fabre told of its
bad character and vicious sting, and it is this ugly wretch—not
any of my favorite "surgeon" wasps—who is generally responsible for the newspaper accounts of wasp stings resulting in violent reactions, and even in death. Here in New Jersey it seems
to have the odd habit of girdling lilac bushes—why, I cannot
say—and in the autumn it greedily eats great holes in the apples of our orchard. Altogether, it is an unpleasant member of
this large family and is to wasps what a starling is to birds: an
unwanted interloper.

The lovely, brightly banded, long-shanked and long-bodied
Mud Dauber, *Pelopaeus*, has had his name changed to *Scelifron*
—no doubt by someone with little appreciation of poetry—
Pelopaeus being, in itself, as euphonious and pleasing a name as
ever has been derived from the Greek.

Pelopaeus (which name, incidentally, is pronounced Pelo-
PIE-us) is such a friendly creature. He (and here again I use
the masculine only in literary form; for it is generally the female
one deals with in studying wasps) has no truck with this crude
stinging business which *Polistes* pusillanimously metes out.
Pelopaeus collects mud, flies home, daubs his nest with much
ingenuity, catches his share of spiders (by stinging *them*, not
me), rams them in, and, in a word, behaves himself.

I recall one incident in which I found good reason to be
amazed by *Pelopaeus.* I had gone to the top of our field to look
for *Pompilus* (a delightful kind of Spider wasp) when, as I knelt
to inspect a tiny burrow, I heard an odd singing. "Singing" it
was, but it was wasp song. I had read of Fabre's delight in it,
but had never myself stopped to enjoy it. There lay, 15 feet or
so away, an area made muddy by a brief shower. In it were a
number of mud wasps, each busily rolling mud into a small
ball which, when just the proper size, would be clasped and

borne away through the air. The singing sound seemed to ema-
nate from a cricket-like flutter of their wings—though it didn't
at all sound that way: it sounded as if they were happily hum-
ming at their work.

But of far more interest to me than their joyous sound was
the "beeline" in which they flew. We have all read of, and
probably seen, the Honey bee, which, when loaded with pollen,
ceases her erratic hunting flight and flies straight home to her
hive. So also does the wasp, but I failed to realize how straight
and precise was that journey.

I noticed, in watching *Pelopaeus* depart, that, under the bur-
den of her pellet, she flew quite low and very straight to a barn
other than mine which lay about 125 yards away. The slope of
the ground to the barn was gradual and entirely devoid of trees,
an open field. By way of experiment I walked some 20 yards
away and looked back to the mud hole. I could see the wasps
leave and come in a straight line for the barn. For amusement, I
edged ever closer to their line of flight until, as I watched them
come along, they passed only inches from my head. Finally I
placed my head directly in their path. I could see them watching
me as they came. Only inches from my head did they waver
and turn in flight, and then continued toward the barn in their
original flight line.

I later cut slender poles and marked the aerial path, making a
"Y" at the end of each pole. In doing so I could see their line
of flight was just as though being shunted down a long glass
tube. Explanations as to how they arrange this within their
tiny heads I leave to the scientists. Check points? Radar? I have
no notion. I am no entomologist . . . but I do see how these men
find joy and satisfaction working among such things. Hardly
are wasps "vile bugs": each is a precision instrument, fully honed
and as complicated as a jet airplane—more so, in fact; we know
what makes a jet fly, but of the wasp we cannot be certain even
as to the design, much less the scheme of the designer.

The heat of July seems to shorten tempers in every direction.
Wasps are not alone in their seeming propensity for lashing out;

other things seem to as well. However, in truth, it has nothing to do with the heat affecting animals; it is the heat affecting us that makes us blunder into the areas near hornets' nests, which, of course, they hasten to protect; to offer provocation to a skunk; or to carelessly handle some animal and be bitten. Of course, to give us credit, it is often difficult to know when we are treading upon ground "belonging" to some wild animal. They cannot put up signs reading "posted." But we should not for that reason timidly keep out of the woods. We are animals, too; it's not their woods alone. And so we must just do the best we can—or be stung, or bitten.

This reminds me of the "ferocious" garter snake. I was walking down the road one day, certainly minding my own business, when I came upon a garter snake. I admired her two ivory stripes and greenish-glass skin and started to walk by. But she was going that way too, and, instead of fleeing as I expected her to do, she (making me recall the Pine mouse) attacked me. She reared up like a cobra and repeatedly struck at my boot. And she kept advancing: this was the curious part. Though I could not have cared less—knowing she was harmless—I tested her by moving slowly backward. She followed, and in a vicious temper. Even after I flicked her over with a stick, she pugnaciously continued to strike and to advance.

Since I had been in the middle of the road, and thus certainly not near her possible young, I could not see how I had trod so on her feelings. I had long known, since a boy, of the garter snake's terrible temper, but I had never seen such a manic display of bad manners. So, not wishing to condone her impertinence, I ended up lifting her on the toe of my boot and depositing her, with a kick, into the top of a viburnum bush. It served her right. Anyone else would have bashed her with a stick.

On these heavy days of midsummer we often see Box turtles (actually tortoises, a terrestrial "turtle"). They plod their unhurried way in, through, and out of the yard as though tomorrow and yesterday were one. The children tired years past of gathering them in for "pets." They eat well enough and make rather nice pets—but there is not much conversation. It fills me with a great anger to see how people fail to swerve away from them as they cross roads. All summer long their crushed bodies are found, covered with flies. A totally useless waste. I have heard many a youthful driver boast of running them down to "hear them pop"—and just once I came upon a callow, bumpy-faced adolescent whose car had run off the road with a flat tire. He was cursing obscenely and whining that he was "only running over turtles" and that the so-and-so turtle shell had spiked his tire. Which it had. "Too bad, sonny," I said, roaring off and leaving him standing there.

We have many and varied kinds of turtles. Being so fortunate in having pond and stream and salt water all in a juncture, we can count many species and quite truly call it "our woods" in which they are found. The Box tortoise is most common, but we have seen the Wood turtle. The Painted turtle—the "pond

slider"—is scarcely ever absent from the pond, while the pretty Spotted turtle haunts our cool, shaded stream. Then there are the Musk and Mud turtles of both pond and streamside. Both are drab, and can hardly be differentiated but by variation in the plastron (the underside of the shell). The salt-water Diamond-back terrapin can often be seen along the edge or out in deep water, where his head is quickly submerged at any hint of danger. Only once did I find the rare Muhlenberg's turtle—and that was, again, in the same Pine Barrens' bog in which I had discovered the orchids. He was most distinctive with his yellow-orange patches on either side of his head.

But the most impressive of all is the Snapping turtle. He is not "mean" with an ordinary meanness—his low-keyed intelligence seems far more primordial and elementally sullen. He has a shell that is quite small, considering things turtle-wise, and he looks rather more an alligator-like creature topped by a ridiculous bit of reptilian armor. Certainly his long, serrated tail is very much like that of an alligator; and his head, with that low, mean air he has, also seems apart from the general run of turtledom. But a turtle he is indeed—and a powerful one.

Our pond is a reasonably safe haven for all creatures now, even for smaller Snapping turtles (for they, too, have their place in a balanced fauna). But a few years ago the scales were tipped most drastically the other way: our pond was a veritable charnel house. The reason was not at once obvious, for one cannot be there to observe all the time, but it was clear something was much awry. Ducks with young would one day be there and the next day gone completely. Other birds and animals were actually seen thrashing about and being pulled down into the pond. Some small boys, seeing this sort of thing, spread tales of a "monster." And—for a change—a small boy was exactly right: some small study of the situation made certain of the presence of a very large Snapping turtle. Undoubtedly he was behind it all—but I was very busy at the time and could not attend to it.

Meanwhile, my friend, R.B., whose lovely house it was that

crowned the pond, became impatient upon seeing yet more ducks disappear. He somehow procured two large turtle traps (I should not have had a notion where to find one) and set them, forthwith, in the pond.

The next day he telephoned me saying, "I caught some pretty good-sized turtles." I said that I would be most interested to see them but was dreadfully involved, and so on. R.B. replied, "Involved or not, I think you'd better have a look." And so I went.

Now, I had seen large Snapping turtles before. I had caught many, one way or another. And I had, yes, seen them "as large as a dishpan." But I had never before seen anything like this. The largest must surely have weighed at least 60 pounds, and the smaller at least 40. The head of the larger was at least 4½ inches *wide!* They were monsters indeed, and, marvelling, I asked R.B. how he'd managed them. He said it was simple, he had only hauled in the trap and shot them with a rifle.

Since the Snapping turtle is probably the most important turtle in the country from the viewpoint of economic value, there (apparently) was a gold mine. But it was on a Saturday afternoon that all this occurred. No fountain of turtle lore could be reached. And on the next day they had begun to draw flies. R.B. buried them. Within a short time the pond was indeed a safe haven, for R.B. kept setting his traps and kept catching Snapping turtles until he caught no more. None was nearly as large as the first, but a few of the "small" ones might well have started some "dishpan" tales on their own. A single rapacious Snapper can do great damage to wildlife in a small pond. It is a wonder we had anything left.

Two years later I found myself musing on the actual dimensions of those turtles. With R.B. helping, I dug for two hours, but he could not recall the exact spot he buried them, and their skeletal remains could not be found. It was of no importance, really, but I was—and am—curious about how large they really do grow. Certainly they had occupied our pond (their pond, really) for many years, and because they have for so many centuries been able to survive and to prosper, it seems quite

likely they will again lay claim to their share of bounty. All this
is as it should be. It was not by whim that the tribal group
from these very woods were called "Unami," the Turtle clan.
They invoked powerful medicine in choosing as a totem this
strong and tenacious animal.

"Let's go to Bahr's" is a family war cry when the kitchen
becomes a bore. Bahr's Landing is a seafood restaurant just under
the "Twin Lights" of the old lighthouse facing the sea on the
Highlands behind Sandy Hook. It is an old and established
dining place, the food is good, and Mr. Bahr is a cordial and
affable host. It is possible to sit at tables where a splendid view
is to be had of Sandy Hook and the Bay.

Clams, at Bahr's, are a specialty. I remember with joy the
waitress's coming with heaping platters of steaming shells on
nights which were cold with a driving snow; her eyeglasses
would be so opaque with vapor that she had difficulty finding
our table. On summer nights like these, clams are still in order;
Littlenecks, this time—cold and succulent on the half-shell.

Clams have been here for centuries, as the Unami kitchen
middens tell us. Even their fossil ancestors can be found high
in the hills. And as we watch from our windows at Bahr's, men
are slowly working over the beds within our sight with clam
rakes, baskets, and the inevitable gray boats. The men can be
seen moving in rhythm with their rakes, and as they move,
waist-deep in the rising tide, they are feeling for clams with
their bare toes in the soft mud.

Even today, as jets circle in their patterns to land at Kennedy
Airport, one can still sit here at Bahr's of a late summer evening
to watch the old clamming sloops slowly tack or lazily go before
the wind. They are low, stoutly built, generally painted gray,
and are not the tidiest things afloat. They are all quite old—as
much as seventy years—are gaff-rigged and of a quaint, old-
fashioned design. If it should seem to you outmoded, in these
times, to use old-fashioned sailing sloops for commercial fishing,
you are quite right. But the government likes it that way. You

see, the quaint little fishing fleet dredges, by government order, only *under sail*. Modern motor dredges could scoop up the entire beds and leave them barren of clams. Now the clamming sloops are fast disappearing from the local scene, but it is not that the government has relented and has suddenly consented to the licensing of a motor fleet. What has happened is that the polluted water of the Raritan River and of Raritan Bay have contaminated the whole of the Raritan basin . . . and so our lovely old clamming sloops are going, not into port or dry dock, but into oblivion.

Many of those remaining still have red sails. Red sails and a lusty, healthy stink of clams. They come in to Belford and to Keyport, followed by clouds of screaming gulls. At least, some used to come in here, perhaps for repairs, for I sometimes saw them here pulled up on local marine railways.

The tidal currents which sweep in front of Bahr's Landing flush out that part of the great bay as a fast yacht taking the fresh salt water "green" flushes and scours its deck. Clams, here, are still edible. But out there and to the north, there is oil seepage and scum-covered flotsam, and they are filling in much of the tidal wetlands for another "Industrial Park."

In the formal garden below my barn (and I have explained to you that I do not own this barn, and that it is "mine" only as a tenant), there is—in its exact center, as would be proper—a pedestal on which is mounted a sundial. Now that sundial, like clamming sloops, conservative dress, morals, and courtesy, is hopelessly out of date and old-fashioned. But it does tell the time and tells it accurately. The pedestal is surrounded by fragrant boxwoods, and foxgloves, delphiniums, tea roses, and Sweet alyssum. And the sundial itself has that gray-green patina which only age and weather can produce.

Such a garden is not simply "planted." "A garden is the mirror of a mind"—and gardens are lovely when they reflect the qualities of graciousness and beauty within the designer. And such encompassing minds as are capable of producing the beauty

of a fine garden are also generally astute in the matter of sundials
—sundials, like everything else, being subject to degrees of quality. Presumably even they can now be had in plastic. Garden sundials are sometimes of glass, often of stone, but most often of
either lead or bronze. They are the focal point of many a
garden, but it is not only in their form and often curious designs,
nor in their telling of the time, that they hold interest, but also
in the epigrams with which they are traditionally inscribed.

I became interested in these succinct little messages many
years ago, and it grew to be a matter of amusement to my family
to see my devious methods of approach in gaining entrance to
strangers' gardens in order to "see the sundial." As my own
interest grew, I learned that I was not alone; that the concise
clarity of these brief messages had, over the years, appealed to
many people. And I found, too, that for the same reasons many
could not help falling into the game of composing these phrases
or couplets for their own amusement.

The grave solemnity of the death of a day urged Dante
Gabriel Rossetti to write:

> *Slowly fades the sun from the wall*
> *Till day lies dead on the sun-dial.*

Charles Lamb wrote, in his "Essays on the Old Benchers of
the Inner Temple":

> *Ah! yet doth beauty like a dial-hand*
> *Steal from its figure, and no pace perceived.*

Chaucer's lines are set thus in a dial:

> *For tho' we sleep, or wake, or rome, or ride,*
> *Ay fleeth the time, it will no more abide.*

Spenser has it:

> *None can call again the passed time.*

And Tennyson, in the "Ancient Sage":

> *Make the passing shadow serve thy will.*

Some sundial mottoes are overly saccharine, as this in an English garden:

> *Ah, far away in some serener air*
> *The eyes that loved them see a heavenly dawn.*

Or pompously classical, as on a Manz dial:

> *Whilst Phoebus on me shines*
> *Then view my shades and lines.*

Or matter-of-fact (as are the Milanese)—from a sundial in Milan:

> *The learned line showeth the city's hour.*

Or, flatly business-like, as that on the dial of the general post office in London:

BE ABOUT YOUR BUSINESS.

Among the most satisfying, perhaps, are the rhyming mottoes, whose gamut of emotions runs the full scale, but which are generally rather solemn:

> *I labor here with all my might*
> *To tell the hour by day or night.*
> *If thou wilt be advised by me,*
> *Serve Thy God as I serve Thee.*
> *Let others tell of storms and showers,*
> *I'll count none but sunny hours.*

John Morton, the English writer, tells of travelling in France with Hilaire Belloc, and of how Belloc invented "the sundial game" in which each of them "made up suitable, or unsuitable rhymes for a sundial." A few of these were published in Belloc's *Sonnets and Verse.* Among my own favorites included with these, are:

> *Here in a lonely glade, forgotten, I*
> *Mark the tremendous process of the sky.*

> *So does your inmost soul, forgotten, mark*
> *The Dawn, the Noon, the coming of the Dark.*
>   and
> *Loss and Possession, Death and Life are one.*
> *There falls no shadow where there shines no sun.*
>   also
> *I that still point to one enduring star*
> *Abandoned am, as all the Constant are.*

But most typically Bellocian (as he is publicly known, at least) is:

> *I am a sundial, and I make a botch*
> *Of what is done far better by a watch.*

Among my own (which I include because, dear friends! one must never miss an opportunity of seeing one's name linked with Spenser, Lamb, and Belloc . . . even if stuck there by oneself!) are these:

> *Though I trace the arc of heaven's course,*
> *I've never learned to ride a horse.*
>   and
> *How sweet this Night; at last away*
> *From the searing eye of Day.*

The sundial in the garden here cheerfully states:

> *I count none but sunny hours.*

I love it—that sundial and its motto—because, I think, I rather feel that way myself.

August

When Foxes Sing

By late July and as August begins, even the most fascinating of attractions in the fields and woods begin to tarnish and grow limp on the anvil of summer. More and more are thoughts and footsteps seeking the shore line and the sea.

In August the normally clear water has become clouded with algae and choked with "sea lettuce" and "Mermaid's Hair," and barnacles, by now, have begun to cling to the boottops and bottoms of boats. Various species of kelp float in on the flood tide, particularly that variety having long waving fronds (*Laminaria*) and also the kind filled with holes, like slices of Swiss cheese (*Agarum*). Rockweed (or *Fuscus*), mingled with the sea lettuce too, at low tide makes a green carpet from littoral line to the water's edge, now far off shore. And among the litter of mussel shells are small bits of Irish moss or *Chondrus*.

At low tide there is a wide expanse of exposed mud flats, covered, as I say, with the green of marine flora. But animal life is nearly as thickly distributed. On pilings of the little dock to which our rowboat is tied there are mussels, periwinkles, sea squirts, and sea anemones. There are stranded jellyfishes, sea worms, and starfishes. Often we can find sea urchins, sand dollars, and sea cucumbers.

The one thing which draws the children away from the white sands of the ocean beach is an expedition to the mud flats of our cove. Their principal delight is in crabs: here is not only something ripe for conquest but an adversary worthy of respect. And to top it all, crab meat is delicious. And so the children join in with enthusiasm.

The chief among our local crabs is the "Blue," which grows to 6 inches "point to point"—meaning across the shell (that is, according to "authorities"—we have seen them bigger). The reason for his complete supremacy, however, is not the meat taken from his shell, but the whole crab—known during its molt as a "softshell." Softshelled crabs are a New Jersey delicacy (as they are elsewhere). Sautéed in butter, the newly molted crab is an epicurean delight. (When Barbara saw what I had written in that last sentence, she said, "And it tastes good too." Never mind, she knows how good they are—and it is hoped that you do, as well.) Still other crabs are found, however: the Calico or Lady crab is pinkish with a mottled design, slimmer than the Blue; Rock crabs live on sand and mud flats as well as rocks. Spider crabs are sometimes seen among the kelp, and Fiddler crabs, with their one greatly enlarged claw and its smaller companion, are common. Hermit crabs that go about with their "borrowed houses" of periwinkle shells, whelks, or moon snail shells, always seem to be comical figures. Horseshoe "crabs" are not crabs at all, although we all think of them as such. These large (to 30 inches in length) marine "crabs" are isolated into a zoological class of their own, the *Merosmata*, and have changed little since the Paleozoic era. And on the sand bars rising from the water where the mud ends are Sand crabs, the small, pink, burrowing crab of the beaches, known to every child with a pail and shovel.

But the big Blue is our local pride. He is taken commercially here, also; and the long cove and creek to the south has many "crab cars," partially submerged wooden cages, which are a sort of limbo between freedom and some really quite superlative dishes. Our own methods of crabbing are: diurnal and on

foot in the shallows with a long-handled net; or nocturnal, in a rowboat with a pressure lamp in the bow, to reveal the crabs lying quietly on the bottom where they can be quickly taken with the net. Often we come home under the weight of an entire bushel of violently objecting crustaceans. But it always seems worthwhile—even though cooking and "picking" is a nuisance. Whichever method is employed, or whatever the time, children are in ecstasy when crabbing is suggested as the game.

Salt-water fishing finds me a rank amateur. Our waters are filled with a wide variety, however. Were I to quote the published list of local fishes annotated by the Sandy Hook Marine Laboratory, it would cover page on page. Of course, some fishes are far more common than others, but it is really the *usable* ones which count. Ichthyology—either sweet or saline—is not my long suit when it comes to intimate descriptions. However, everyone who lives on this littoral "pasture" is conscious of one aspect or another of the tremendous harvest that the sea affords.

Like most things, our fish (and fishing) are seasonal. At different periods of the year one or another thing is "in." My own propensities are most definitely toward a gustatorial outlook. It may be highly "unscientific," but as I see it, ichthyology is splendid—but it can be even better served in a sauce and garnished with parsley. And so, the ova of *Alosa sapidissimi* I salute in the spring as Shad roe; the adolescent *Pomatomus saltatrix* I revere as baked "Snapper" (the Bluefish); and our local *Paralichthys dentatus,* or Summer flounder, fresh from the salt water and plainly sautéed in butter, is near perfection. I have consumed Dover sole both at Dover and in Dieppe—and it is succulent beyond belief—but our good local flounder is a near equal. It is with bursting pride and sober gratification that I can say of my children that they are adept, perspicacious, and most singularly adroit in the pursuit and capture of all these gastronomic delights. We live well by the sea. *Deo Gratias.* (And *Gratia Scientifica* and *Salve Poseidon,* besides; this is not a dilution of faith but a general sprinkling of good wishes— which, like holy water, fall cool and refreshing upon the cheek in summer and certainly have never done harm to anyone.)

The children also fish up out of the sea a number of what they call "trash fishes," such as the Toadfish, which swallows their hooks; eels, which make a tangle of their lines; Sea robins, rays, sharks, Puffers, and assorted, small "bait robbers" of different varieties.

Of the odd sorts of other fishes, there are mullet, croakers, porgies, grunts, mackerels, hake, whiting, and whatnot of interesting things that are accidentally caught from time to time.

One of the most well-known commercial fishes is the Menhaden or "mossbunker," upon which is centered an entire local fishing industry. At Belford (on the bay shore) is a giant processing plant which has a great fleet of very large trawlers. There Menhaden are taken from attendant small boats sent out from the trawlers to lay purse seines, and the returning fleet steaming north just beyond the breakers is always an interesting and familiar sight from the beaches on summer afternoons. The fishes are not edible, but are processed for oil and for fertilizer.

A more-or-less recent innovation in local fishing has been that of skin diving with a spear gun. Most of the true *cognoscenti* disdain "scuba" equipment and prefer the use of the simple mask and snorkel. Certainly, they catch fish, and—like the archer—they do it cleanly, leaving no wounded behind. To the best among them the only real challenge is the Striped bass, which is truly a noble fish and worthy of their respect. They will also take the Blackfish, or Tautog, which is also good eating, though not on a par with the great basses.

On one occasion I was fortunate in being able to accompany some of our most renowned divers and spear-fishermen. It was in late September and down the coast some miles at Shark River Inlet—our own waters being not nearly as clear at that period. We dove to a depth of 25 feet, and I was astonished at the numbers and varieties of fishes to be seen. Since I had been diving on the Great Barrier Reef of Australia, in Tahiti, and in Bermuda (although at all times in an amateur fashion), I was prepared to be disappointed in northern waters. It is true that the brilliance and clarity of tropical fishes were indeed missing, but in their place was a tremendous range of variations of blues, grays, yellows, and greens. Even white was subjected to odd light refractions which gave it as wide a scope of attraction as a bright color. I saw shimmering schools of small northern barracuda, Blackfishes, and Croakers near the pilings of the bridge, and great schools of species which I could not identify. It was an enthralling experience.

Later in the same day I accompanied my friends into the surf, where one of them shot a very large Striped bass. My own fishing there was unsuccessful—first, because I was a novice anyway, but also because of the sand sent swirling by the surf; I found that seeing anything in the opaque void was nearly impossible. My friends hunted mostly by ear and taught me how to listen for the loud *whumph!* made by the Striper's tail as he turns suddenly and forces the water as air is forced in an explosion. But although I heard a great deal of *whumphing,* I saw nothing of any bass.

Under the instigation of the underwater sportsmen, a new interest has been taken in the shore and ocean life of the Jersey coastal strip. Interested laymen, cooperating with the Sandy Hook Marine Laboratory, are now working toward the preservation of species and of their natural breeding grounds. So-called "fish counts" are being taken, in which lay fishermen are a great asset to the scientific personnel involved in this phase of oceanography. The Sandy Hook Laboratory itself has become a full-grown oceanographic institute, with large ocean research vessels and the most modern in scientific equipment and staff. This growth is of especial interest to me, for I was among the nucleus of interested parties who saw Dr. Lionel Walford launch the first designs of the laboratory in its earliest stages. It is still

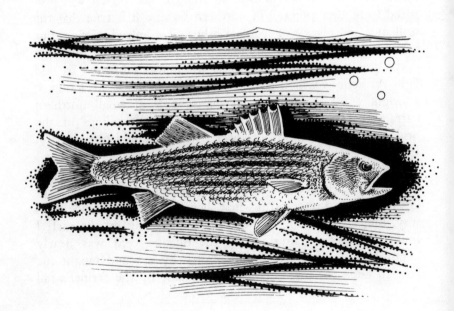

growing at a rapid pace and is already numbered among the major centers for oceanography in the country.

Golfers who play regularly soon learn about moles and the constant efforts made by country club staffs to rid them from the areas near the greens; and there is another sport in which the players come up against a "problem" with natural history. That game is tennis. Perhaps the problem is not universal, but I have seen it before.

That "problem" at our nearby club is wasps. Or rather, in any other place it would be a problem. I have told you before of *Sphecius*, the Cicada-killer. It is nothing if not *big!* An inch and a half doesn't sound big—at least not until you are cognizant of its being an inch and a half of striped wasp, buzzing and bearing down on you. I have already let the cat from the bag in having told you its sting is reputed to be not all that bad, but people in general are slow to be convinced of this (as was I). At our club there are some numbers of grass courts and the rest, now, are of the new composition material. But the old courts that adjoined the grass were of a fine powdery clay and the edges of the paths are still of clay. This clay is a most favored housing material for *Sphecius*. She digs her holes, goes off to kill her large Cicadas, and comes home with them paralyzed, clutched under her belly. Of course, the paths are filled with the comings and goings of the players. The odd point of the story is that here is a whole segment of people—athletically inclined, but still a representative group of plain people—who, instead of panicking at the sight of these great wasps, have been over the years "conditioned" to their presence. No campaigners arise to "get rid of the wasps." There is no hysteria. Visitors are informed that the wasps are harmless (they are), and everyone—including the wasps—goes about their business peaceably. The velvet loveliness of the green courts, against which the white attire of the players in motion vividly stands out, is a sight that is refreshing. But especially refreshing—to a naturalist—is the sight of a splendid species like *Sphecius* "belonging" in a human community. This certainly comes under the name of "adult education."

I have often been concerned over this problem of people's reaction to various things about them in nature. My concern has not been particularly with the preservation of, say, "un-popular" animals like bats, spiders, snakes, and, generally, the "things that go bump in the night." It has been with the kind of education that has failed to impart truth. At which point in life do fears and aversions to other living creatures present themselves? Not at the breast, certainly? But often pre-school maternal influence is strongly felt, as are elementary school years. Here these prejudices are formed. But it doesn't stop there. Quite regardless of the degree of advancement in educa-tion, these prejudices persist. How often I have heard from really quite intelligent people (otherwise), "But I can't help it —I *still* feel that way." Well, it is my opinion that they don't "feel that way" at all, but that they think they should. People often seem to have a blind spot in their make-up for certain things. They can invent and operate computers, unravel the secrets of chemical compounds, or trace the helical bonds in a strand of DNA, but they will say, "I hate spiders."

Why in Heaven's name, do they "hate spiders?" The answer is that they don't. They could learn about spiders in half an hour and—except that they would be forced, perhaps, to stop from time to time to marvel—they could put an end to such spider talk. But they don't *wish* to know of spiders. Spiders, they think, are not worth knowing about. And they will be-come most defensive in backing up their theory. Grown men, proficient in both the theory and form of argument, will say, "But I just don't *like* them, that's all." What is it that instills this deeply ingrained nonsense? I have no answer to any of it.

What I do know is that spiders are neither wildly spectacular nor at all abhorrent. They are simply eight-legged arachnids going about their business. And their business is no more nor less than everyone else's—including your own—procreation and survival, a bit of rest in the sun, and an interest in a job well done. Spiders, in spite of their "image," are really quite docile. They are ferocious only in the pursuit of their proper business, and with little of the rending of propriety that we see on Madison Avenue.

The spider with which we are most familiar is the House spider, *Theridion*. It is this spider that is responsible for some "cobwebs" in dark corners—but the spider is only liable to account for a sticky web; you must accept responsibility for the dust which adheres to it. They are quite small—only ¼ inch long—and are rather drab and dusty in appearance. If you should have an abhorrence of spiders but find, too, that you have cobwebs, then you will have to accept the fact that you have lived comfortably with spiders for probably quite a while, and that it is a little late for an hysterical objection to their presence. They feed on other insects, such as flies and moths, so their presence can be—and is—beneficial. This information, however, I am sure, will fall upon deaf ears; cobwebs and spiders must *go*. And it will be a tidy accomplishment if you can do it, for the House spider is a persistent creature.

Also, *Salticus*, the Jumping spider, is another interesting house spider; he makes no snaring web, but literally jumps after his prey, letting out a thin life line as he goes through the air, on which he climbs back to safety. It is he who makes the long streamers of single-strand cobwebs: they are his old life lines, left hanging. (The dust, again, has no relation to the spider.) *Salticus* is a harmless and really quite amusing creature if you will stay to watch him.

Other spiders are less obnoxious, perhaps, because we seldom see them. The tiny Balloon spiders, *Erigone*, are fascinating to me for, although they quietly spin their tiny webs on the ground and are themselves so small and inconspicuous (body only 1/20 of an inch long), they travel by climbing high to a treetop, spinning a long silken strand, and then "ballooning" high up and away into the air. The Funnel-web spider is also interesting, building his nest of closely compacted gossamer and shaping it like a funnel. You will find him in your lawns, as do we. The Wolf spider, *Lycosa*, you will find less amusing, for they grow to rather a good size (to ¾ inch in body alone; encompassing nearly 2 inches when their eight legs are included). Again, this is another spider which does not make a nest, but, wolflike, runs rapidly in pursuit of its prey. It is harmless and beneficial —but will undoubtedly never prove popular because of its size and quick, elusive actions.

The Orange garden spider, *Argiope*, also grows to great size; at least the female grows to a full inch, while her mate is only one-quarter her size. She is spectacular, not only in her black and yellow-orange coloration, but in the remarkable intricacy of her great web, which is engineered with miraculous skill each night. With these strong nets she "fishes" for quite large insects—even large moths and grasshoppers. The web is extremely strong and often as much as 10 feet in diameter as anchored, although the main "catching area" is perhaps only 2 or 3 feet wide. In New Guinea, while walking through the jungle, I have often been stopped in my tracks by walking into the great web of an allied species, the so-called "Bird spider," so named because it actually does catch small birds. Its web is so strong that it takes quite an effort to push through, and the strands are like heavy threads. Our own Garden spider is noteworthy, too, for the strong strands of its web; but mainly it is in the geometric perfection of its workmanship that we find room—even if grudgingly given—for a true admiration.

We have no large Tarantulas or Trap-door spiders here in New Jersey (except sometimes in places like Hoboken, where they are brought in on banana boats from the tropics). But we do have, most commonly, the Black Widow spider. We have them under our porch, in our basement, and in the hen house and barn. But so also, most likely, do you. Please don't be shocked: for this spider has been the victim of the worst reputation imaginable. It has been maligned so badly—mainly by a sensation-hungry press—that the stigma will never be wholly eradicated. Certainly it is "poisonous"; all spiders are. So is too much aspirin poisonous. The possibility of your demise issuing from a Black Widow's bite is probably far less than your choking to death on a piece of roast beef. This is not because the spider *cannot* be dangerous, but because, generally, it will not. The *Latrodectus* (which is its name) must normally be forced to bite, and even then provocation must be extreme. They are related to the House spider, the females being shiny black with a scarlet "hourglass" on the ventral abdomen. And they are quite "menacing," if you will believe the newspapers. But don't believe a word of it.

If you should be disturbed by my telling you that you undoubtedly shelter Black Widows, please do not be alarmed. It is like my telling you that you cook over gas (if you do). It is a simple truth about which you should feel no anxiety. But neither should you turn on that gas without lighting it. Thus with Black Widows; they should not be provoked. It is a mistake ever to go out of one's way to eradicate anything in a temper, but to quietly engineer its removal is perfectly logical and generally simple. Stamping on something in terror is often a dangerous game, possibly giving you a heart attack, if nothing else. My daughter has often come in saying, matter-of-factly, "I found another Black Widow spider and took her and her eggs on a stick into the woods."

Actually, spiders are really quite timid. Their menacing attitude is merely a being at-the-ready in the lawful pursuit of their livelihood. Step on them and harry them if you will, but they have their place in the natural order: so should it be with all who mind only the business that is theirs, and let everyone else be content to mind his own.

Beetles are yet another "repulsive" insect to many who are ignorant of them. The numbers of varieties and their multiple forms and activities cover a wide range, but many are predaceous on insects and often do a great deal of good. On the other hand, certain of them do a great deal of harm—so that is certainly no plea for their preservation. Many are quite beautifully colored, principally in the hard shell or "elytra," the tough, hardened forewing which serves to cover the membranous hind wings used in flight. Among the most brilliant are the Tiger beetle and some of the leaf beetles. Among some of the most exotic are the Long-horned, Stag, and Rhinoceros beetles; and some of the most destructive are the Japanese beetles, other leaf beetles, and the weevils—and millions of dollars in damage is done each year and millions more spent in combating them. But they should not be thought of as "repulsive"; here again, they have a proper place.

In popular opposition to such as spiders and beetles are summertime's butterflies and lovely moths. The Swallowtails, tiny hairstreaks, anglewings, and fritillaries are known by every schoolchild, as are the Luna, Polyphemus, Cecropia, underwings, and Hawk moths. They are not only charmingly patterned, but their colors are either brilliantly painted or soberly but attractively subdued. Always they are popular and pleasant to see.

My entire point in speaking of these things is that, in great profusion, each of hundreds of varieties of insects are part of our daily scene here in the country. It must be said that many are to be found in New York City proper, as well. But it is here that they all fit with little conflict, one adjacent to the other. In no less a parabolic harmony than that in which the earth swings in orbit, all of these things I mention—rotating in small parabolas of their own—seem in no collision with each other nor with anything else. An occasional rising-up to do battle against one segment or another of its teeming population has little effect upon the whole of this company. That is why I, personally, at least, think little of the prejudices attaching themselves at random to one creature or another. It simply seems unfair.

The waning of August makes for some hideous nights. It has nothing to do with heat, but with noise. Ordinarily our woods are quiet; one is able to hear even the distant surf or to listen to the soothing wind through the oaks. But toward the terminal days of August the foxes begin to sing.

"Sing" is really hardly the word. But that is what they think they are doing, at least. We've seen them often, sitting dog-fashion, head thrown back and nose to the sky, yapping and howling for all they're worth. The sound? It has been described more ways than nearly any other wild sound. It is, perhaps, somewhere between a bark, a cry, a cough, and a sneeze. To me it sounds like a high-pitched cough which sometimes cracks. But I once met an old-timer who said it sounded halfway between a "baby being strangled and a eunuch sneezing backwards." And he may well be more nearly right than I!

Our hypothesis for this sudden increase in vocal entertainment —and I am certain we are correct—is that now the cubs are half-grown and beginning to learn the ways of foxdom. That is, they are into their own version of the "Screech Owl School." We are certain of it for, although we can see little after darkness falls, we lie awake in bed and trace their actions by ear.

The principal area of activity is the hen house. Ordinarily, as I have said, the adult foxes leave it strictly alone. But each year the young, half-grown cubs, "full of beans and twice as sassy," are struck with the brilliant idea that this hen business would be a pushover. And so they flat-footedly sally forth to the hen house and straight into the mouth of a large dog. The dog knows little else (since greyhounds have a brain case the size of a golf ball), but she has come to know of foxes. She lies low, and gives them every opportunity to make fools of themselves.

They begin by creeping forward on their bellies, in good, sound, fox-fashion. But they go too fast and too recklessly. And as they go on, the parent foxes—sensible enough to stay well out of range—begin a parental tirade of disapproval the like of which only parental concern can create. The young foxes, like the fools they are, yap back. As they close in on the well-locked chicken house, the parents grow quite angry, even to coming in themselves to try to cut the young off from their follies. And about this time enters the dog, loudly complaining of foxes and streaking for the no doubt horrified cubs until her long chain just saves the intruders. Bedlam continues to ensue when the elder foxes try to bring the cubs together again from all points of the compass. Then we hear the young being persuaded to stay together in a gaggle, not without an occasional nip in the flank to show who's boss.

Night after night passes and we come to know the voice of each adult and even to differentiate between the cubs. They can be heard going through a whole curriculum of "do's and don'ts" until, finally, the cubs' voices grow deeper, they absorb more of the lore of caution, and they begin, as the autumn begins, to emerge into more adult and—thankfully—more quiet foxes.

September

Fruit Flies in the Applejack

The coming of September is unheralded by any particular thermal changes. It can be just as hot and dry as August, just as deep in summer green. Somehow, it is not what it *is* that makes the infant September different, but what it is not. It *looks* the same, but isn't.

Suddenly one is reminded that the swallows have long been gone, that many other birds are behaving strangely, and that each day someone else "disappears." The deep foliage prevents our knowing when they go, many of them; but go they do. This same foliage is now dusty and tattered, having been racked by summer showers and blown by summer winds. The leaves look old, and hang limply from their branches.

The departing birds of which one takes particular notice are the shore birds. All summer there have been terns and gulls and various other breeding species, but now a great many shore birds are to be seen: sandpipers, plovers, willets, yellowlegs, godwits, and occasionally a curlew. One of my favorites is the Golden plover, but it is always rare and appears, seemingly, only after easterly storms—its normal migratory path being over the open ocean. It flies, as most of us know, from the northern tundra to the limits of southern South America, farther than any other bird in the world. The Black-bellied plover is a regular migratory transient, coming often to our cove.

Among other shore birds (commonly called "peep" by the knowledgeable among observers) which I particularly like and constantly watch for are the Red Knot, the Purple sandpiper, the Dowitcher, and the Ruddy Turnstone. None of them is excessively rare: it is just that I am rather fond of them all. I have, over the years, seen a very great many rare birds—even including the vagrant Ruff from Europe—but I don't make a fetish of rarities, enjoying the common ones with equal zest. During each month of the year the Sanderling patrols our open beaches, as does the Red-backed sandpiper (the latter sometimes being seen in large flocks); but each of these, too, is present in greatly reduced numbers—even to single individuals—during some months of the year. But in September, they are all here, it seems, in shimmering, wheeling flocks—always a joy to see.

The shore birds are among the first of the hosts of migratory birds, but soon they are followed by every other winged thing that forsakes the north during winter. They come singly at first, then in groups, and finally in teeming legions along the Atlantic coastal flyway, like coal through a chute. Birds thus concentrated permit opportunities for study that ornithologists employ to their advantage. Of all the migratory research stations on the coastal flyways, few are so carefully organized and painstakingly operated as that just 45 miles south of here at Island Beach. Mrs. Stanley S. Dickerson leads a large team of volunteers who operate the station on a twenty-four-hour-a-day basis from August through October. The migrating birds are captured in nets of fine silk mesh, carefully identified, measured, weighed, banded with an identifying aluminum ring, and released. The numbers of birds so banded in a single season has reached the staggering total of over 25,000! This kind of research is of extreme value to scientists who are working on obscure facets of bird population expansion, insect control, migratory limits, meteorological effects, and divers other technical problems having to do with bird life.

It is interesting, also, to note that, through the cooperation of Elise Dickerson and her staff, new facts are being uncovered as well about migratory bats. It was long suspected that migrating bats flew much the same routes as did birds, but not until eleven Silver-haired bats were captured in one night was it definitely proved that not only did bats of this species fly as do many birds, in closely packed groups, but also that they fly in, with, and amongst the birds in their nocturnal flights.

Both birds and bats, then, are flying together this night as I watch for signs of them across the wide face of a brilliant harvest moon. But on this night, I see nothing—only, with my binoculars, the barren craters which dot that far-off orb which, it seems, has become so important that man must explore it with his foot as well as his eye. Well, perhaps some good shall come from it . . . but in the meanwhile

> common living is a burden, and earnest men are at siege upon us all around . . . they are building hotels (I hear) in the place where Acedes discovered the Water of Youth in a hollow of the hill Epistemonoscoptes.

The harvest time is now truly upon us, and, since this is called "The Garden State" (by edict, no doubt, of some ambitious politician who somehow smelt Gain), there are things to be put into jars, into the freezer, and to be enjoyed fresh from the vine, the orchard, and the garden.

Barbara's jelly bag in these days is in perpetual sight, swinging in the warm breeze, and tempting wasps from every direction. Freezer bags and boxes waiting filling are knocked onto the floor, picked up, secured, and then swept off again as peelings fly, fruits and vegetables are blanched or stewed, and jars are sterilized and lined up in steaming rows. The combined aromas are devastatingly inviting, and fingers are poked into things, then tasted and nursed with the tongue when the fruity porridge proves too hot. The thick, warm residue of scum in the grape pot is scraped out with a wooden spoon and fought over by the milling children.

The same bounty which comes to us also comes (but not by

our intention) to many of the wild things about us. The grape
arbor and the apple trees are nightly filled with a zoo-full of
raccoons, possums, and Flying squirrels, while the ground under
them is thickly populated by skunks and foxes, all with cheeks
bulging with fruit. Under the arbor the stains of juice and the
carpet of discarded grape skins are disgraceful.

Last night, as there perennially is, there was yet another
raccoon fight in the apple tree outside the kitchen. The racket
and caterwauling that goes on is frightful as each greedily attempts to see that no one else gets more than himself. They
quarrel and bicker and drop apples in a *plunk*ing staccato, until
late into the night. I went out at ten o'clock with a light, since
the moon was behind a blanket of cloud, and shone it up into the
low branches. Two young coons noisily scrambled away, but
the same fat old patriarch who haunts our feeding tray simply
sat there on the branch—his muzzle stained with grape juice
and his mouth filled with apple—and looked back at me. Even
my laughter failed to daunt him, and as I stood there he again
began chewing and licking his chops in complete and utter

disregard for me, the light, Arthur Goldberg, and the massed pipes of the Black Watch (Mr. Goldberg was speaking from the television set and the children were experimenting with the phonograph). I went into the house, turned off Mr. Goldberg, silenced the Black Watch, and reached for a book. But the sounds of animal gluttony still filtered in from the outside darkness.

The harvest of the sea, as well, is brimful at this time of the year. New Jersey, however, is less noted for the ocean's bounty, perhaps, than are other states. And perhaps it is a good thing. The state of Maine would seem to have a steel grip on the minds of most people in the matter of lobsters, as Vermont surely has cornered most of the maple-sugar market. Here in coastal New Jersey, at least, maple sugar is in scant supply . . . but lobsters are another thing entirely. Even at Pedersen's Sea Fare (the establishment of a local Dane who, from hauling in nets from his boat, has arms like knotty tree trunks) hang signs advertising "Fresh Maine Lobsters," because people insist on them. And what they are getting is Maine lobster shipped in by rail and by truck. That which is eaten by Mr. Pedersen, however, and by us, and by anyone else who knows better, is New Jersey lobster. Certainly they do not come from the sandy flats of the Navesink nor from Sandy Hook, but they are truly local nonetheless.

Off the coast are certain "reefs," not of coral, but of rock. Every fisherman knows of them and fishes for Blackfish from boats anchored over them. Mr. Pedersen knows of them as well, and not only fishes near them but sinks his lobster traps among their crevices. The lobsters he catches are much cheaper in price because he cannot sell them, in truth, for "Maine lobster"; but they are the same species and are every bit as succulent—and any talk to the contrary about Maine's icy water, beds of kelp, or whatever, I am prepared to dismiss as nonsense and to offer proof in the event of dire necessity (which last is economic caution and not a dilution of conviction). Our lobsters are scant hours from the ocean floor when we present them to the pot. And the best way to cook them is at the beach of an evening, over a driftwood fire, boiled plainly in sea water taken up with a pail from the surf. Only melted butter is needed in addition to New Jersey's own lobsters. A bit of fresh corn, roasted perhaps, and clams steamed over seaweed—and whatever is necessary of liquid to make a man whole—these, also, are not to be despised . . . but they can only add to the grandeur of the boiled lobster, as such. *Rex nascitur, non fit.*

Each year there is an influx into these woods which arrives as surely as does the solstice. At one moment the woods will be empty, and in the next they are filled with shadowy Italians. The Mushroom Pickers have arrived.

Each with his basket and his bag, these furtive gnomes are far from the laughing, exuberant Italian I have come to know— quick of wit, filled with gaiety and heartiness; striking their breasts or heads in expostulation; flinging out their arms in a loving, ursine embrace; or breaking through laughter and through tears into boisterous song. These Italians are much different. They are dark, squat, cowering, and unsmiling. That is, they are all these things until you get to know them. They are furtive because they have grown used to being thrown off land, running from the police, seeking anonymity in quiet dress, and gaining access by stealth.

What is their crime? There is none. They come seeking wild mushrooms because they know—and we do not—the many that are not only edible but really quite excellent. In other words, they seek that which we cannot use, or will not use. They do no damage, leave no trace. They only come quietly, spend their day in the aromatic woods gathering their elusive fungi, and as quietly leave. But each year at this time the police are summoned, cars are seen stopping to listen as they pass the woods, and more than one poor gnome has been made to empty his baskets into the woods.

It is true that there is a good, sound, Italian word for "trespass"—*trasgressione*—but it is obvious that none of these men know it. But that is not the point: it is that they do no harm. It is perhaps disconcerting to ladies alone in their houses to see men apparently lurking in the nearby woods, and of course trespassers should be checked on. But I have always been staunchly on the side of these "bandits and brigands" whom everyone so fears.

It took a long while for me to gain this confidence; but once I did, the suspicious "gnomes" became genuine people: Angelo Ruffini, Ugo Pignatello, Joe Russo, and—my old and good friend—Patsy Pisani. Patsy used to take me along with him to patiently teach me the various kinds of mushrooms one could safely gather and those which must be avoided at all cost. It was strange to hear his complete familiarity with these, "our" woods. Beyond a doubt they were his as well. Patsy was not young—but he told me how his father showed him this place many years ago. How, twenty years ago, there had been a special tree—"here" (and sure enough, there was the rotted stump); and that "there" (and he would point) was a very old log around which grew another kind of mushroom in rare profusion. He told me of having watched our arrival thirteen years before, and of knowing my dog—and yet for years we were unaware of his presence.

I was taught how to find all the mushrooms and how to pronounce the name of each—not in Italian (as I have since learned) but in Sicilian and Neapolitan dialect—some being roughly hewn words of a friendly but often intimate nature. I was instructed how to prepare and to cook them all, as well. But I shall not describe to you what I have learned, nor draw for you any sketches of these native fungi—for my talent in recognition or in illustration might be mediocre, and mushrooms are nothing for the amateur. In fact, in spite of my complete schooling, I find that each year I must yet question Patsy as to edible varieties . . . and I have more than once been proved wrong.

When I think of these men I cannot help but be saddened by the thought that still (in spite of my pleas to the contrary) people regard them with disfavor and suspicion. I think of their cars, poked into the shelter of covering bushes, filled with long loaves and wine and boxes of tomatoes, garlic, and cheese. There are flat packages of *prosciutto*, and onions. There should be songs and laughter in our woods, but, after all these years, there are no songs left in them. I think of poor Mrs. Pisani (who is generally not allowed in on this man's game), and how she stood for hours alone beside the car, while the men went off in bachelored, garlic-reeking splendor—and she told me in rare patches of English that she so wanted to come, "just to see the leaves." So she just stood there for hours, looking so sad and so old in her black dress, her fat old ankles, bowed legs, and turned-over wide-heeled shoes. She would never have spoken to me at all, of course, but for Patsy having told her I was "all right." Nor would she come to the house, even with Barbara's prodding—and later, when we brought her some biscuits and tea she wept with embarrassment, so shy was she. She told Barbara how to cook "Mama Fungi," the great, cabbage-sized tree fungus.

I have eaten many kinds of our native mushrooms—under Patsy's directions (and they are remarkably different, one from the other, and remarkably good)—but when one is not an Italian and versed in such things, mushrooming can be a quick way to a most Unhappy End.

I must now tell you the "Story of the Electronic Dog." I caution you that this is not out of Erle Stanley Gardner—but out of our own woods.

Now that autumn is again upon us, the hunters are back at their poaching, their running of dogs, their usual athletic high jinks in the woods. During this week, last September, there was a rainy spell, with much dampness and a low-hanging fog which lasted for days. We knew the hunters were active, for their dogs were running in packs and would set up a tremendous howling from time to time.

Now I, certainly, am not against shooting, or allied with any

group damning hunters—except that I do object to their cutting
up our coons to feed their dogs. In fact, I really feel mellow
enough about poaching, which has to it a sporty aspect that is
lacking in mere trespass. My only purpose, really, is to preserve
these woods intact for a latter-day populace who will—by that
time—be appreciative of any wild thing left to them. And so I
make an effort, at least, to protect all of the wild things living
here; foolish of me, of course, because it cannot be done. And
on top of it, I have no more real right to "protect" them than
others have to shoot them. But I go through the motions by
seeing that hunters are given no opportunity for filled bags.
Thus there regularly ensues a generally comic scene of "Key-
stone Cops" in action. No one is hurt, no one is prosecuted or
fined, but complete license to kill everything in sight (as is
often done in many places) is denied. And we must be winning
out—for our woods are filled with a very fair share of ecologically harmonic (if a bit lardy, at times, as with our old coon)
wildlife.

The incident concerning the dog began with the usual din of
baying up and down the hills. Then a large, handsome hound
bounded out of the laurel and into the yard. And I bounded
after the dog—for the rules of this cops-and-robbers game we
play demand a *corpus delicti* of some sort, and a canine one is
allowable and proper. The rules would have me contact the
local constable, who comes, attaches dog to leash, and waits at
the police station until the owner retrieves dog, paying two
dollars. This two dollars for a lost dog is his "ticket," evidently,
for going right back into the woods in less than a week. In
fact, more than once I have phoned the station saying, "Old
Bessie is back," and the reply has been, "What, again! She was
in last week!" And so it goes. The reasoning behind the whole
farcical procedure is that before long the hunters will tire and go
elsewhere, giving us a long respite.

This time the dog's collar said "Gussie." She was friendly
enough, but went through the house like a drunken tractor.
And, besides, she was soaking wet and steaming and smelled

"doggy" to the point of ripeness. So she was put into the kitchen, which (if you will recall the seal) can be hosed down. She commenced to howl at first, but after a biscuit quieted her she seemed inclined to wait for the policeman in quiet resignation.

We had noticed that her collar had some sort of wire attachment but thought little of loosening it, especially since it seemed to do no harm—and besides she stank too much. But all of a sudden she gave a yelp of terror and shook violently. Minutes later, she did the same thing. And yet again.

We began to grow nervous: she *was* still slobbering at the mouth and was wet and shaking. But no, her eye was clear. But she obviously wanted investigating.

As I tried to loosen the collar I too gave a howl and virtually leapt through the air.

"What on *earth* is the matter with you?" asked Barbara.

"I've been *shocked*, damn it!" I exclaimed in no small temper.

"Oh, nonsense," Barbara purred, "what over, bad reviews?" And then the dog gave another leap and another cry, while at that moment the policeman came into the kitchen.

I gave him a heated summary of my encounter, while he, bending over the dog, said—after the fashion of policemen the world over—"Now, what's all this?" And then *he* gave a great leap and a yell, saying, as he landed, "Holy Christ Almighty!"

Together we held the dog and yanked off the collar, and there—having been hidden in the thick fur—was a little black box; and from it extended the foot-long piece of wire, obviously an antenna. Also, a blunt copper nail an inch in length extruded itself on the inside of the collar.

"Well, I'll be damned!" said the officer. "An electronic dog!"

And she *was*. We concluded that it was some sort of training or calling device, used instead of loud cries or whistles to call back the dog. Perhaps it could turn her right or left, or make her bark or not bark—who knows? We considered that the dog, too, might be a robot—but her consumption of biscuits seemed to nullify that reasoning. Whatever the device, it must have been that the dog's excessive wetness had increased the electric charge, for though it was in reality a mild shock, a shock it was, just the same.

One of the boys became obsessed with the idea of rigging the old hound with lights and electric bells and setting her loose, and actually took it to the bell stage by attaching the wires to an electric house bell. The owner—on the other end of the radio-sender—seemed to be seized with apoplexy, for the collar rang and rang while the dog and policeman ate homemade cookies (the Swedish kind with sugar sprinkled on top), and we all laughed ourselves into exhaustion.

And then the dog and the policeman left, the latter holding the collar gingerly by its strap end in one hand; and in the other, the dog lead and more cookies.

"Good night, Bert," I called.

And Bert yelled back, "It sure ain't ever dull out this way."

Now, as many of the leaves are just beginning to turn and on the back porch are bushel baskets overflowing with apples, we are reminded that golden autumn is truly here again. Have I said that this is my favorite time of year? I probably have. Autumn . . . and apples.

Applejack is a New Jersey drink. Never mind, now, about telling me of Calvados, or that you know of a tidy little distillery in Tasmania. I know full well that apple brandy is nothing new. But applejack is the best apple brandy of all. I once pointedly waded through six different brands of French Calvados and a Spanish apple brandy one fine winter to give proof to my premise. There is more than one brand produced here as well: but Laird's is the best. There is no inclusion of either peel or core, as is done in France, just pure apples. The distillery is only seven miles or so away, hidden in a hollow of the inland apple orchards on the way to Freehold. It is the oldest family-owned distillery in the country and, though small in comparison to some, is well known and respected, even exporting applejack as far away as the Philippines and Germany. Laird's, to me, means "home apples" (even though they import some of theirs from Virginia), a purely local thing. A distillation of "home" things.

Applejack—with a bit of juice from the tropical "key" limes —is a drink of the finest sort. Applejack smells of apples: it *is* apples, our own good apples. And we are not alone in thinking it fine. As I walk in the cool of evening, after dinner, into the garden, and as I return with my empty glass, I am followed by a cloud of *Drosophila*, the ubiquitous fruit flies so useful to geneticists. Even indoors in midwinter, somehow the fruit flies find my glass. Now what better advertising might you wish than *that* for a New Jersey drink?

Epilogue

...A Return to October

There is a great deal more I might say. Does it matter that it is really no longer "the Country" but only, as I say, another view of the City? Does it really matter what it is *called?* There are the same foxes and coons, White-footed mice, and, generally, the same old cast of characters. To us, with each succeeding year, it is like comfortably settling back, yet again, for a performance of *Swan Lake* or *Giselle*—seen a dozen times before. But one must live here to feel that way.

The children are in a tree house high on the west hill. They have a perilously hung rope ladder which they tell me adults cannot climb. (And I believe them, for the ropes are the old lines from our ancient catboat.) They shout down to me that they can see further than I ever could imagine. Youth usually can. From where they are, up there, they can see far out to sea —and a great deal of New Jersey, besides. I suppose it is as well I don't climb up there. Somehow the view would seem to belong to them.

What of this megalopolis of which they speak nowadays? What of the further encroachment of "City Life"? What of the *New York Times* article about the new home of the Metropolitan Opera at Lincoln Center: . . . "It is near the site of the old

Somerindyke Farm in the Village of Bloomingdale, where the Hudson was alive with fish, flocks of passenger pigeons would darken the sky and the hunting was good." What of dire prediction and gloomy forecast?

Not a word from me.

Today I walked a country mile. I kicked through the leaves newly fallen from the Silver maple in front of the barn. The new "barn squirrel" seemed to take a more kindly view of me. I saw a chipmunk.

And this afternoon I pedalled to the post office on my bicycle. (That steel grid on the old iron bridge always gives me the willies.) There were Ring-billed gulls in the marsh, and a warm breeze came from the sea. You could smell the salt.

About the Author

Russell Peterson is a naturalist, illustrator, and author who has been a staff mammalogist with the American Museum of Natural History in New York and has led scientific expeditions to New Guinea and north central Australia. Well known as an authority on bats, he is equally recognized as a writer who can lend an aura of lightness and charm to the exacting complexities inherent in scientific research. He is a member of the American Society of Mammalogists, the Australian Mammal Society, and the Explorers Club.